# Light i
# Place

Encountering Depression

*Light in a Dark Place – Encountering Depression*

By: Carlton Coon, Sr.

Copyright – 2019 by Carlton L. Coon Sr.

Unless otherwise noted quotations are from the King James Version of the Bible.

Editing:  Pam Eddings

Graphics:  imagiwildinc at Fiverr.com

ISBN-13:  9781797823003

*Printed in the United States of America*

*Dedicated to Norma J. Coon*

*You know more about this topic*
*than any person should have to know!*

*Thanks for being there in some long and difficult seasons*

# Table of Contents

Pre-Release Reviews of *Light in a Dark Place* ..................................7

Introduction..................................................................................11

Section I The Shadow that Sits Heavy.......................................15

Chapter 1 Invisible Yet Intolerable..........................................17

Chapter 2 The Mind is a Curious Thing..................................25

Chapter 3 Situational or Major Depressive Disorder.............29

Chapter 4 Depression in the Bible............................................31

Chapter 5 Impacting People Have Battled Depression...........39

Chapter 6 Why Is Depression Such a No-No? ........................45

Chapter 7 Movie Sets and False Fronts ...................................49

Section II The Substance Behind The Shadow .........................51

Chapter 8 Diagnosing Depression ...........................................53

Chapter 9 What is A Depressed Brain? ....................................55

Chapter 10 Caution: Bridge Out ...............................................59

Chapter 11 Imbalance..................................................................61

Chapter 12 Depression's Cost ...................................................63

Chapter 13 Not in Control ..........................................................67

Section III Strategies to Survive Depression............................71

Chapter 14 Decide to Fight It .....................................................73

Chapter 15 Simplify Your Life....................................................77

Chapter 16 Mapping an Unwanted Journey ...........................83

Chapter 17 Look Behind the Green Screen ..............................87

Chapter 18 Was a Blacksmith Ever Depressed?......................91

Chapter 19 Get Outside.................................................97

Chapter 20 "Be Prepared"...........................................101

Chapter 21 Don't Make Unnecessary Decisions ...........109

Chapter 22 Vitamins for Mind & Emotions.................111

Chapter 23 Pray – Differently......................................113

Chapter 24 Seek Counsel.............................................119

Chapter 25 The Sound of Music...................................127

Chapter 26 Someone Else's Problems...........................131

Chapter 27 Clean Up, Dress Up...................................133

Chapter 28 Tom Barnes' Advice - Talk to Yourself.......135

Chapter 29 Medicine for the Mind...............................138

# Reviews of *Light in a Dark Place*

Carlton Coon has opened his heart to the hurting minds of many. I have been a friend who has walked with him through "dark tunnels". The phone calls, hearing his voice on the other end saying, "Pray Roy, I'm going into a dark place," was more than enough to make me stop and pray. I made it my mission and ministry to be the friend who would stay in touch, make him laugh over something funny, and take the wheel to steer him through those dark moments in his life. This book will be like a medicine to you so you can offer this helpful healing prescription to others.

Roy Barnhill
Bishop – The Pentecostals
Lumberton, NC


*Light in a Dark Place* is a brutally honest appraisal of depression and the effect it has on the sufferer and others. As one who has suffered from depression since my early teens, I believe this book can be an immense help. Unfortunately, many think that if you are a Christian, you should not suffer from depression. Sadly, this is not always the case.

Vivienne Imarisio
Church Administrator
Brisbane, Australia

This book brings to light a subject that has been in the dark corners of the church too long. This light is not overpowering. It is thought-provoking and well balanced. There is a blending of solid scripture and science. This book offers an intelligent and practical way to encounter depression. There is help here that assists those who struggle with the disease of depression.

Scott Breedlove, MS, CPS, MARS
Church Planter – Jefferson City, Missouri

*Light in a Dark Place* validates the experience of depression. As a former counselor such a validation is the first step toward finding help.

Melissa Fross
Church Planter
Quebec City, Quebec

*Light in a Dark Place* is much needed. I have never seen such wonderful information from any Apostolic writer. The words written here are true and can help many.

Derald Weber
The Pentecostals of Lafayette
Lafayette, Louisiana

None of us have it ALL together...only God does! I remember when a family member was battling depression. I had the attitude of *'suck it up and get over it.'* In time, I realized there were factors I was ignoring. I hope others read this book and find an answer to issues they thought they would never face. Thanks for being brave enough to help those who struggle with depression.

Bruce Howell
Global Missions Director
United Pentecostal Church, International

It took only minutes in this book for me to realize just how deep and dark depression is. I was taken aback by the list of traits alone. Until now, I had no idea depression affected people in those ways. Pastor Coon is transparent and writes from experience, not theory. Most important: *Light in a Dark Place* references the infallible Word of God.

This book was not written to break into the literary world. This author has already written over 25 books. *Light in a Dark Place* will help people, particularly people of faith, who are affected by depression, both directly and indirectly.

Suffragan Bishop John Fonzer
Pentecostal Assemblies of the World
Sr. Minister - New Bethel Apostolic Assembly
Moss Point Mississippi

I never understood depression until I read the opening sections of *Light in a Dark Place.* I now have a bit of a grasp on behavior exhibited in some people. Depression is explained in an understandable way from the factual and spiritual perspectives!

Chairman Ronaldo Togle
Apostolic Jesus Name Church of the Philippines
Iloilo City, Philippines

*Light in a Dark Place* shines the light of hope into a dark world by courageously confronting the stigma of depression with practical, biblical advice through the lens of personal experience.

Bryan Parkey
Missouri UPCI District Superintendent
St. Louis, MO

*Light in a Dark Place* is thought-provoking and mindset-changing. It addresses a subject not to be ignored, or "spiritualized" away. The author has become personally vulnerable in an effort to help. This book helps one understand this very real and complex issue, and how to help. A "must read."

Pastor Zane Isaacson
Whitehall, Arkansas

Depression is often talked about in the shadows due to the misunderstanding attached to it. *Light in a Dark Place* sheds light on depression. The author's insight to help people with depression opens a doorway of hope. This book is a *must read* for anyone who wishes to understand or is going through depression.

William Sleep
Quebec Men's Ministry Director
Montreal, Canada

In his book, *Light in a Dark Place,* Carlton Coon addresses a subject that is often mischaracterized by Christians. In a familiar, frank, and transparent style, light is shed on areas of mind and emotions. The clearest voice comes from one who has been there. This book is a *must read* for any who suffer from Major Depressive Disorder. I would also recommend this book to any pastor to gain a better insight into how to help those who fight depression.

Rev. Art W Schnitzer
FAC Maryville Outreach Director/Facilitator
ALJC Missions America Church Growth & Resource Director

Many hide their depression behind a cloak of secrecy. The battle rages from sadness to suicidal thoughts. *Light in a Dark Place* exposes a real enemy by one who at times has walked through that dark. For all who have been looking to understand and get some help with depression, this book is for you. It is brief, concise, and on target.

Stan Thrift
Author/Evangelist
Jonesboro, Louisiana

I was asked to review a few chapters of *Light in a Dark Place*. I ended up reading the whole book. What I was supposed to do that day went unfinished. The section on fighting depression fascinated me. It offered the same mechanisms I've used to survive my battle with childhood trauma.

Lance Meyers
Bible Teacher/Pastor
Tulsa, Oklahoma

I appreciate the openness and honesty found in *Light in a Dark Place*. We need to hear that. I also love the true life stories of the famous, politicians, preachers, the folks mentioned in scriptures, etc. who battled depression. The book gives a well-rounded approach, proving that depression is not new nor is it for those who have "sinned" or are worthless.

Steve Drury
Director of Stewardship Ministries
United Pentecostal Church, International

# Introduction

Soon, my effort on the topic of depression will be seen as naive and lacking in depth. Some may view it that way immediately. Other books will supersede *Light in a Dark Place*. I'm hopeful this happens. Just now, someone has to crack the door on dealing with depression.

As I've talked about and written of my experiences with depression, many have contacted me by phone or email. Others stop me at various events to share their story.

Ministers and the spouses of ministers speak of depression *confidentially*. In whispers people say, "I struggle. I was diagnosed with depression. I take . . . . for depression." Whispers are not healthy. We need to talk about depression!

*Light in a Dark Place* is intended to:

- Give a minimal education regarding depression. My personal experiences do come into consideration.
- Bring the topic of emotional and mental health, into the light of day.
- Validate the reality of depression.
- Help depressed people embrace Jesus' compassion and find Him as the source of hope.
- Offer practical insight into surviving the darkness of depression.
- Ring a bell of hope, for both time and eternity. Depression can be survived.

My medical knowledge is limited. The information in *Light in a Dark Place* is not intended to be a substitute for professional medical advice, diagnosis or treatment. These thoughts are for information only and are based on personal experience. Always seek the advice of your physician or another qualified health provider with any questions about your medical condition and/or current medication. Do not disregard professional medical advice or delay seeking advice or treatment because of something you read in *Light in a Dark Place*.

This book includes unsophisticated and inconsistent references and bibliography. My footnotes would not pass muster for a master's degree.

I've had the opportunity to see life from many angles. With over twenty-five books in print, I may have a bully-pulpit to expand the discussion about depression.

My wife and I are acquainted with a lady who has quit on life. She is like someone Luci Freed speaks of in *A Time to Heal*, "Because of the overpowering and oppressive nature of depression, some people believe that it is somehow their lot in life."[1] The lady I'm talking about has decided that living under the heel of depression is God's will for every day of her life.

She has accepted a lie. No person should accept life controlled by perpetual depression. She should not see depression as her lot in life. None of us should. Depression is not a final destination, even if it is a life experience.

## Decide to Fight!

A person can move through depression, if they don't surrender to it. Here is a grand thought - don't surrender. If you don't quit – you win!

Revelation 12:7-11 tells of a war in heaven. Michael and others of the Lord Jesus' angels are shown fighting against a dragon. The dragon represents satan or satan's emissaries. The dragon and his angels are said to have *prevailed not* (KJV).

As John saw it, satan's dragon will go to war, but the dragon will not win. Greek scholar Kenneth Wuest expanded the phrase *prevailed not* in this way, "The dragon and those who followed him did not have the power to win out." The dragon will have the ability to do battle, but will not have the power to win. The only way the dragon can win would be for Michael and the angels to surrender. Surrender is not an option for Michael or for you.

View depression as your dragon. If you keep fighting, the dragon cannot win the war. You may lose some battles, but one battle does

---

[1] Freed, Luci, and Penny Yvonne. Salazar. *A Season to Heal*. (Nashville, TN, Cumberland House), 1996. P 76

not make a war. Don't surrender to the dragon of depression. There will be days when you are overwhelmed. You may join Job in ruing the day of your birth. Tomorrow is another day. Fight!

Those who stay in the battle eventually win. The war may not be over until eternity – but you will win.

## Balancing the Discussion on Depression

Being extreme on any life issue is generally dangerous. Extremism is certainly dangerous when considering emotional and mental health. At times, conservative Christians have demonized mental health professionals. Some mental health professionals may deserve negative press. Many do not.

Emotional and mental trauma can be part of life. Several friends have equipped themselves to help others with such seasons of life. Counselors, family therapists, psychologists, or psychiatrists are not all tools of satan.

I've needed help battling depression. Many others have needed help. Some people who read *Light in a Dark Place* won't accept my observations. Though you don't agree, please keep what you read in mind. Though depression is not wished on any person, there will likely be a day when your grandchild, mother, or a strong and mature saint will battle the dragon of depression. What you have read here may be of help as you try to try to bring light to their dark place.

# Section I
# The Shadow that Sits Heavy

The shadow called **depression**, prevents you from speaking out.

The shadow called depression becomes your only friend.

The shadow called depression is lying. (TheMighty.com)

# Chapter 1
## Invisible Yet Intolerable

Some people never seem to even be downhearted. In *Happy Holidays*, the story is told of two church elders. One was always "up" and expressed difficulty in understanding why other people, "let themselves become depressed." The man simply did not have a problem in that area.

Another elder in the same church, suffered frequent bouts of despondency. His business life was stressful, and he internalized those feelings. He also struggled with conflicts left over from childhood. Both men were committed to their church, and genuinely loved other people. Yet, one often experienced depression while the other managed to cope with whatever setbacks came his way.[2] Both were good men with significant influence. The man who did not fight depression was not better or stronger than the other. He simply had a different sort of life path to walk.

Illness is generally hidden within the human body. The symptoms are not. Pain is felt though there is no physical trauma. This is true of appendicitis, kidney disease, gallstones, cancer or a headache. People sick with these conditions do not wear a cast or walk with a limp. The invisible illness still disrupts their life. An invisible sickness tends to be more destructive than a broken bone that requires a cast.

In a similar way, depression is an invisible pain.

- Depression is as real as a migraine headache.
- Depression may be as destructive as kidney disease.
- Depression can destroy – productivity, healthy relationships and result in a loss of life.

Novelist William Stryon wrote, "Depression is a true wimp of a word for such a major illness."

---

[2] Minirth, Frank; Hawkins, Don; Meier, Paul. *Happy Holidays – How to Beat the Holiday Blues* (Grand Rapids, Michigan; Baker Book House, 1990) P. 26

## What's It Like to Be Depressed?

It is hard to describe depression fully. Each person's experience is different. But there is a universal trait: <u>while enduring depression, nothing comes easy</u>. Every single act and decision requires more effort than normal.

Jack Dreyfus founded the successful Dreyfus Mutual Fund empire. Dreyfus fought depression. He recalled trying to explain to others about his depression. "It is almost impossible to convey to a person who has not had depression what it's like. It's not obvious like a broken arm, or a fever... It's beneath the surface. A depressed person suffers a type of anguish which in its own way can be as painful as anything that can happen to a human being. His brain permits him no rest. His mood is low; he has little energy, and can hardly remember what pleasure means."

During depression, "The wonder and awesomeness of being alive slowly erode. We find ourselves slipping into a gray mood, then a long 'flat' stretch in which not much appeals to us." [3]

Words fail, but here is a start on what it is like to be depressed. Some reflect my experience. Other observations come from what others have gone through.

- Getting a car in gear, and turning it around usually happens instinctively. Depressed people have to think about each step.
- Life is gray and cold.
- Visiting an ATM - only not being able to remember the PIN. The same PIN used for decades.
- A "black cloud" hanging just over my head.
- "Watching your own feet," thus minimizing eye contact.
- The shower is a place to cry with nobody the wiser.
- Losing interest in self-care. Why shower or shave? Why dress up for the day? Even if I did, it wouldn't matter.
- I feel flat.
- Desperately alone.

---

[3] Hazard, David, *Breaking Free From Depression* (Harvest House Publishers, Eugene, Oregon, 2002) p. 5

- Everything is drab, lifeless, and tired.
- A black hole.
- When reading, by the bottom of the page, I cannot recall what I read at the top of the same page.
- My days are dark.
- I am numb.
- I am in slow motion. Everyone else is at hyper-speed.
- The word or phrase needed in conversation or while speaking to a group - just won't come.
- Following a conversation is a challenge. The ability to concentrate is not there.
- I am unable to move, both literally and figuratively.
- I am my own worst critic. Put an "L" on my forehead for loser.
- Self-hatred.
- Mental self-immolation. It feels like my brain is on fire.
- Anger turned inward.
- I go to bed tired and get up tired!
- An unknown season of intense doubt.
- My enthusiasm is at best feigned.
- Malignant sadness.
- Phone calls are not answered, and calls go unreturned.
- You grocery shop late at night. There is less likelihood of running into someone you know.
- The dishes pile up in the sink.
- Feeling despicable, stupid, and unlovable.
- To smile, even at a grandchild, requires conscious thought.
- Feeling less and less capable of making good decisions.
- Agitation is often near. There is anxiety about what is happening. I lash out in anger because I'm anxious.
- A gray monster lurks within.
- I have no energy.
- Walking, waking dead.
- My desire for anything, even things I really enjoy is gone.

- I died a few weeks ago and my body hasn't found out yet.[4]

A child told her depressed mom, "You act like you are dying." The child was not far from correct. The mother acted like she was dying because emotionally, she felt as though she was dying. Lack of sleep, and in some instances a constant flow of tears indicate that life is horrid.

Depression has a wide-ranging impact. It affects body, mind, spirit and soul. As a culture, we seek a quick fix. For depressed people, there is seldom a quick fix.

Thinking is slowed, and mental acuity is distant. This is one of the more horrible aspects of depression. Without your normal mental resources, the world is frightening.[5] In depression, something is out of balance. The wonder and awe of life and living are gone.

**Depression Has No Logic**

Depression is irrational. Grief, hardship and disappointment can cause some traits described earlier. Grief is a normal and healthy process following any loss.

A study clarified the differences between grief and depression. The one major difference: Those battling depression struggle with self-denigration. Grief does not cause a person to feel bad about themselves. They feel pain over their loss. People who are depressed will often have a sense of worthlessness.[6] This sense of worthlessness is a major identifier for depression.

Depression is different in another way. Depression happens contrary to the concept of cause and effect. Depression may have no easily discerned cause.

My life has been full and fulfilling. Millions of people would love to trade stories with me. Our family enjoys good health. People read my books and listen to my sermons. Don't misunderstand; my life is

---

[4] Solomon, Andrew. *"Anatomy of Melancholy,"* The New Yorker, January 12, 1998 P.54

[5] Welch, Edward T. *Depression: Looking up from the Stubborn Darkness* (Greensboro, NC; New Growth Press, 2011)

[6] Kramlinger, Keith M.D. (Editor in Chief), *Mayo Clinic on Depression*; Mayo Clinic Health Information; Rochester MN. P. 7.

not a fairy-tale. There have been disappointments and personal failure. But on balance, no reason comes to mind to explain me ever being depressed.

Yet, for decades I've battled *depression*. For decades my experience was identified as "clinical depression." In recent years, the terminology has changed. Mental health professionals tell me the present term is Major Depressive Disorder (MDD). With that in mind, MDD or Major Depressive Disorder will be used for the remainder of this book.

A person struggling with depression may then be classified as Mild, Moderate, or Severe. A person who had "clinical depression" would today be given a diagnosis of Major Depressive Disorder; Severe. Regardless of the terminology, when at its worst, this condition colors the entire world.

The darkness of depression could define my life. I don't plan for that to be the case.

## Depression Deteriorates Life

Depression causes life to deteriorate. *Physiologically*, depression slows the metabolism. It lowers the body's immune response and weakens resistance to disease. *Spiritually*, depression cuts a person off from the awareness of God and His presence. We lose the sense that God is present.[7]

A depressed person misses God-moments because such moments are not seen for what they are. Depression leaves people exhausted, hurting, and hopeless. Offering gracious hope and help to such people, whether saints or sinners, should be part of the mission of the New Testament church.

## Depression is Common

Millions of people battle Major Depressive Disorder (MDD). It is said that 1 in 4 people who attended church Sunday was struggling with some level of depression.

The late Tim LaHaye wrote several books and booklets on depression. He also provided seminars on overcoming depression.

---

[7] Hazard, p. 14

LaHaye wrote, "During the past few years, I have taken polls in audiences totaling at least 200,000 people. In each poll, I've inquired, 'Is there anyone here who has never experienced depression in his entire life?' Not one person ever indicated, that he has escaped the problem."[8]

The preacher who preaches to such hurting people will never lack for a congregation. The commonness of depression reflects the observation of Joseph Parker, a British pastor in the 1800s. Parker said, "There is a broken heart in every pew."

## Depression Does Not Happen in Isolation

Depression is a family illness. In varied degrees, the presence of depression affects every person who lives at an address. If one person in a family is dealing with depression, the impact is unavoidable. The child who said her mother acted as though she was dying was experiencing depression alongside her parent. Those who live with someone battling depression, will also suffer.

If you have a depressed family member, you may want to shake the person, or scream at them, *"Snap out of it."* My family members were never that harsh – though there were times when they communicated their frustration about what was an untenable situation.

People who were not family members have used such techniques trying to "heal" me. They did not work. Instead, they tended to make my life even darker.

## Foundational Responses

If you have a family member who is depressed, pray for yourself and for that person. You will need grace! Pray for the person's healing. Pray for your patience. Pray for wisdom to understand how to prevent the depressed person from becoming irresponsible. When a person stops fighting depression, it can produce what the late inspirational writer Zig Ziglar called a "loser's limp."

---

[8] LaHaye, Tim, *Ten Steps to Victory Over Depression*, (Zondervan Publishing; Grand Rapids, MI, 1974) P. 9

Second, if you have never been depressed, realize that you have no point of reference for what your family member is experiencing. An elder who had a hearing problem said, "When someone is blind, others are sympathetic. But if a person has a hearing problem, people are irritated." People respond to depression in the same way. If you have a heart condition or thyroid difficulty, there is sympathy. Depressed people don't receive that same level of sympathy.

John White warned that we should "be cautious of judgmental attitudes toward men and women struggling beneath the weight of depression, and of glib and inaccurate explanations of their condition . . . the godliest of men and women have been gripped by profound depression."[9]

If a person has high blood pressure, ulcers or some other disease, people are sympathetic. Those conditions may even be caused by depression. But if depression is mentioned, people have a tendency to say, "I don't know what you have to be depressed about. You should be grateful for your blessings."[10] Don't make that statement. Such statements harm more than help.

Instead, seek the ability to see beyond the moment. God is interested in your family's situation. He is listening.

The book of Revelation tells of golden bowls that hold the prayers of the saints, (Revelation 5:8). Perhaps all you can do is pray for your family member. Pray on. Be as the woman whose importunity got the attention of the unjust judge. Pray again. Jesus treasures prayer. As you fight this battle alongside your family member, remember, "Your high priest can be touched with the feeling of your infirmities," (Hebrews 4:15).

Depression is not weakness, laziness, a lack of will, or a character flaw. Depression is a disease.

---

[9] White, John, *The Masks of Melancholy* (Downers Grove, Illinois; Inter-varsity Press, 1982) P. 63

[10] Maughon, Martha; *Why am I Crying* (Zondervan, Grand Rapids, Michigan, 1983). P. 72

# Chapter 2
# The Mind is a Curious Thing

My first encounter with brain chemistry involved a woman connected with a former pastorate. One day, I received a panicked call from the lady's daughter. Her mom, who was always careful of her appearance, was acting strangely. Earlier that day, while at the grocery store, she had begun disrobing.

The people with her took the lady home. While they were not paying attention, she escaped. As she ran through the neighborhood, she again began disrobing. As she ran and disrobed, she was cursing non-stop.

I visited the home to pray. One of her children warned me, "Mama is out of her mind. We can't keep clothes on her, and there is no telling what she may say." When I walked into the room, the lady recognized me and welcomed my prayer. While I was there, her children had to do battle to keep her covered. We all prayed for her. I walked out of the room, with nothing having changed.

Within a day, the woman was institutionalized. As often happens with such situations, all went rather quiet. Her family was embarrassed by their rather conservative mother publically disrobing, and screaming curses.

A few days later, I encountered the woman in the same store where she had disrobed. I was shocked and surprised to see her. A daughter later explained that a blood test had shown a chemical deficiency. A substance necessary to the proper function of her brain was almost totally lacking. Doctors began immediate treatment. Within hours, she was normal.

That experience helped shaped my understanding of the human mind. The human body is an amazing, yet curious organism. We are truly *"fearfully and wonderfully made"*, (Psalms 139:14). Scientists remain amazed at our attributes. Research will continue to expand the understanding of just how wonderful God's creation was. Of all the components making up our body, the mind is the most amazing. The brain is also the least understood.

The lady, whose story I've told, was not dealing with depression. A medical/chemical/biological solution to her strange behavior gives credence to the significance of how a natural, normal biochemical impacts the mind – and our behavior.

There is much to indicate that some depression is the result of certain chemicals being inadequately available in the brain. If our pancreas or appendix can be sick - why not our brain? Would anyone leave the lady mentioned earlier in her madness, because we resist the idea that the brain would ever need help? Could we not apply the same kindness to help a person dealing with depression?

## Defining Depression

Depression is defined as a sad feelings or loss of pleasure lasting for two weeks or longer. These feelings are accompanied by at least three or four other depressive symptoms. The net effect is a person having some disruption in their ability to function at work, with their family, or to fully enjoy life.[11]

Like many medical situations, depression develops over time. The severity varies. A person can feel "down" and lacking in energy for a few weeks. Or, depression can leave a person feeling hopeless and unable to function. In time, the feelings lift, and life returns to normal.

So why depression? There is no simple answer. Several things can come into play:

- The chemistry of the human body.
- A person's temperament and personality.
- Environmental influences such as a person's upbringing or whether they have experienced abuse.
- Repeated stress can deplete needed brain chemicals. There is much research regarding adrenal fatigue syndrome's effect on depression.[12] Constant pressure wears down the body, spirit, and emotions.

---

[11] *Learning to Live with Depression*, (Developed by Medicine in the Public Interest; Boston, MA., President Louis Lasagna, 1994) P. 4

[12] Biebel, David B. and Koenig, Harold G.; *New Light on Depression*, (Harper Collins, New York, NY; 2004) P. 51.

- Sinful behavior that produces an incongruity between the ideal self and reality.
- Learned Behavior
- Post-Traumatic Stress
- An inclination toward guilt and shame, instead of being receptive to mercy and grace.
- Genetics
- Accepting responsibility for aspects of life beyond a person's control.

Though there is a common experience in depression, there is not a common cause. The way each person stumbles into depression – or is blindsided by it – is unique.[13] In some, if not all instances, several of the factors mentioned may compound the likelihood of dealing with depression.

## Fearfully and Wonderfully Made – BUT not Always Healthy!

As noted earlier, our entire being is fearfully and wonderfully made. God-created, natural chemicals within the body and brain to manage our behavior. These biochemicals affect our appetite, sleep, and motivation. Illness comes if our system is not creating the biochemicals in correct amounts

An example is those who consistently overeat, feel hungry even when their body does not need food. Why does this happen? Certain biological and chemical systems have been incorrectly trained to simulate a feeling of hunger.

The body's biochemicals are necessary for health; including mental and emotional health. During times of depression, the necessary ingredients may be confused, not working properly, depleted, out of synch, or perhaps not speaking to each other.[14]

Lorin Bradbury pastors in Bethel, Alaska. He is also a psychologist. Pastor Bradbury is well-respected in the mental health field. He has served in several roles of leadership in Alaska's associations of mental health professionals.

---

[13] Welch, *Depression* Kindle edition: Location 226 of 3524.
[14] Keen, Bonnie; *A Ladder Out of Depression*. (Harvest House Publishers, Eugene, Oregon; 2005), p 52.

Pastor Bradbury observed, "Researchers can chemically induce depression in a test group. This being true, it would certainly seem to be accurate to say that in many cases, 'Depression can be the result of chemical imbalance in the brain and body.'"

Depression, whatever its source, is no respecter of persons, pedigree, history, or position. Depression happens in good families. Depression happens to the religious and the irreligious. Depression may come to a parson, a backslider, an atheist, or an infidel.

The greater goal for those who suffer depression is to give them hope and direction.

# Chapter 3
# Situational or Major Depressive Disorder

Many things happen to bring a person down. I've only known one person of whom it was said, "He never had a down day." It may well be that the one person did a good job of hiding moments of despair. Situational depression differs from the depression being addressed in *Light in a Dark Place.*

## Situational Depression

If you wreck your car, get fired, your house burns down, hear a bad report from the doctor, or your dog dies, you will likely feel quite low. Depending on the severity of the situation, this low feeling can meet the criteria of a Major Depressive Disorder. It is not. What we experience at such times is grief.

This situational depression is being blue, in despair, or depressed about a specific situation. When the situation resolves itself, whether that is soon or not, it is likely the low feeling will go away. Often the person will not experience depression again.

## Major Depressive Disorder = More than the Blues

Major Depressive Disorder is not the same as the low times caused by the death of a loved one, or a medical condition such as a thyroid disorder.[15] MDD may occur when a person does not have a negative situation. The person struggling with depression may have received a promotion, bought a new home, or received a great report from the doctor. Yet, that person enjoying great success, suddenly struggles with deep despair. MDD depression can be illogical. It is not connected to any particular occurrence in life.

A song the Carpenters made famous said, "Rainy days and Mondays always get me down."[16] What the song describes is not MDD. Another song sung by Kenny Wayne Shepherd conveyed, "Everybody gets the blues sometime . . ."

---

[15] (https://www.mayoclinic.org/diseases-conditions/depression/expert-answers/clinical-depression/faq-20057770Posted May 13, 2017 Read 12/27/2017)
[16] Williams, Paul H., Nichols, Roger S.; Song; *Rainy Days and Mondays*, 1971.

Major Depressive Disorder is quite different than the despair over losing a job. Depression is not having several bad days because your boss is on a tirade or your children are sick with the mumps.

Please realize that there is a difference between situational depression and a Major Depressive Disorder.

# Chapter 4
# Depression in the Bible

Depending on where you are in life, you may not need to read this chapter. The optional chapter is included to communicate emotional struggles within the Bible. If you are already aware of this or are otherwise convinced, move on to the next chapter.

The Bible contains an honest historical account of men and women heroes with "warts and all." People making bad decisions fill the Bible. But, the greater picture reveals the story of Jesus' mercy and ability to help.

It is good that the Bible lets us see people who are not at their mental and emotional best. It offers hope to all who struggle in a similar way. The Bible translations I'm most familiar with never use the word "depression." However, symptoms described leave me thinking great men and women of the Bible battled depression.

Depression is not always the sign of a broken relationship with God. Instead, the depression of Elijah, Abraham, Paul, and others demonstrated their humanity. They dealt with the same emotional burdens we carry.

## Job

Scholars believe Job was the first book of the Bible put to pen. Job is introduced to us as a good and Godly man, who soon faced an extreme attack by Satan. You probably know the events. Grief at his loss was the fountain from which Job's depression flowed. Again, a distinction is needed. Major Depressive Disorder is not necessarily attached to a loss such as Job experienced. But, there are words and phrases in Job that give understanding of what depression feels like.

Job was not distant from God. He was well respected in his community. Yet, Job's success and intimate place with God did not protect him from a pit of despair.

Job's words are those of a good man. His confusion and misery are obvious. The difficulties came from every direction - physically, spiritually, mentally and emotionally.

Job 2:13 tells of the arrival of Job's friends to comfort him. However, the shock of Job's appearance was so great that they all wept and sat in stunned silence for seven days and nights. At this point, Job is hanging on by his fingernails to survive. He has nothing to say. Job's silence is characteristic of depressed people. Often, they retreat into the quiet.

Finally, Job broke the silence and cursed the day he was born (3:3), and wished himself dead (3:11). The best man on earth is having a colossal breakdown. Job's loss was beyond imagination. Many who battle depression show the same behavior as Job.

Job's monologue continues in Job 3:20-26. Perhaps it was prayer; maybe Job is talking to his friends, or he may have even been talking to himself.

Job's words are the language of depression. Depressed people use these sorts of words, even when they have not suffered Job's terrible losses. The underlined words denote Job's state of mind.

*20 Wherefore is light given to him that is in misery, and life unto the bitter in soul; 21 Which long for death, but it cometh not; and dig for it more than for hid treasures; 22 Which rejoice exceedingly, and are glad, when they can find the grave? 23 Why is light given to a man whose way is hid, and whom God hath hedged in? 24 For my sighing cometh before I eat, and my roarings are poured out like the waters. 25 For the thing which I greatly feared is come upon me, and that which I was afraid of is come unto me. 26 I was not in safety, neither had I rest, neither was I quiet; yet trouble came.*

**Job 3:20-26**

Job did not quickly regain emotional balance. In time, Job's friend, Bildad, accused him of being presumptuous. In answering the accusation, Job's response communicates his unfulfilled expectations. Job had expected certain things that did not happen. Job complained,

*He [God] destroys my hope like a fallen tree,*

**Job 19:10**

"Destroyed hope" is another term that describes depression. Being frustrated with God is another common trait of those battling depression.

Job also spoke of his search for God.

> *8 Behold, I go forward, but he is not there; and backward, but I cannot perceive him: 9 On the left hand, where he doth work, but I cannot behold him: he hideth himself on the right hand, that I cannot see him:*
> **Job 23:8-9**

Like Job, depressed people feel abandoned by God. This abandonment has not really happened, but the feeling is inescapable. Making matters worse, the one longed for and not found is the Redeemer Himself. Through the dense fog of depression, God cannot be seen. Job used words a depressed person uses.

God is not available. God has turned His back. Why bother going on in such a state? If God has abandoned me, I'd just as well join God and turn my back on myself too.[17]

## Naomi

Naomi's story is told in the book of Ruth. Due to famine, Naomi's family had left their home village of Bethlehem. Naomi, her husband, and two sons immigrated to a neighboring country named Moab. While living in Moab, Naomi's husband and adult sons died. Eventually, the now widowed Naomi returned to Bethlehem.

Naomi returned to Bethlehem empty-handed. Her former neighbors greeted their old friend. Her response to them was,

> *Call me not Naomi, call me Mara . . .*
> **Ruth 1:20**

This is a play on words. Naomi means *pleasant* while Mara means *bitter*.

Naomi's instruction, " . . . *call me Mara,*" was not spontaneous. Naomi had been thinking about who she was. How many times had Naomi silently said, "I've got the wrong name. There is nothing

---

[17] Welch, *Depression*. Kindle Reader: location 189 of 3524

pleasant about me?" What Naomi told the people of Bethlehem was well rehearsed.

The words communicated Naomi's anguish. She saw herself as a bitter loser. The woman returning from Moab had a self-definition of *bitter*.

Like Naomi, depressed people label themselves negatively. The harmful thoughts constantly rattle in their mind. The negative becomes that by which a person self-identifies.

Those battling depression are self-deprecating. Naomi saw herself only through the lens of loss. She ignored the fact that her daughter-in-law, Ruth, had chosen to accompany her to Bethlehem. Naomi had become a significant influence in Ruth's life.

> *16 And Ruth said, Intreat me not to leave thee, or to return*
> *from following after thee: for whither thou goest, I will go;*
> *and where thou lodgest, I will lodge: thy people shall be my people,*
> *and thy God my God: 17 Where thou diest, will I die,*
> *and there will I be buried: the LORD do so to me,*
> *and more also, if ought but death part thee and me,*
> **Ruth 1:16-17**

Naomi's self-centeredness was counter-intuitive. Naomi did have a bitter testimony. But, the bitter testimony was the story of her past. In the present, something positive was taking place. Naomi's self-absorption caused her to overlook her impact on Ruth.

The most helpful thing Naomi could have done for herself or Ruth was to put the attention on Ruth.[18] Instead, depression kept Naomi's focus on herself. MDD creates a universe consisting only of the depressed and his pain.

### David

David, is called a man after God's own heart (Acts 13:22). He is named as the author of seventy-six psalms. David's psalms, and those of others, are transparently honest. Many of the psalms

---

[18] Sanders, J. Oswald; *Facing Loneliness* (Crowborough, East Sussex, England; Highland Books, 1988), P. 161.

repeatedly show someone struggling to gain emotional balance. As you read the following words, remember their source.

*Why art thou cast down, O my soul? and why art thou disquieted in me? hope thou in God: for I shall yet praise him for the help of his countenance. O my God, my soul is cast down within me: . . .*
**Psalm 42:5-6**

*Why art thou cast down, O my soul?*
*and why art thou disquieted within me? . . .*
**Psalm 43:5**

Anyone who has lost hope can relate to these feelings. While we cannot say David suffered from a biologically caused depression, the anguish and darkness he *voiced* sound similar to someone suffering from a depletion of certain chemicals in the brain.[19]

Imagine a contemporary response from those who are not willing to admit to God's people having emotional struggles. *"Hey David, you wrote, 'The Lord is my shepherd, I shall not want.' What happened to you? It seems like you are lacking a lot right now. Have you lost your relationship with God? You need to go pray through."*

Was the writer backslidden as he wrote,

*" . . . the enemy hath . . . smitten my life down to the ground;*
*he hath made me to dwell in darkness, . . .*
*Therefore is my spirit overwhelmed within me . . .*
**Psalms 143:3-4**

Some might say, a real saint never has the feelings expressed in any of those Psalms.

Someone I can't properly cite said it well.

Depression is
Debilitating, defeating,
Deepening gloom.
Trudging wearily through

---

[19] Mohline, Dick and Jane; *Emotional Wholeness – Connecting with the Emotions of Jesus* (Shippensburg, PA; Treasure House, 1997), P. 90-91.

The grocery store,
Unable to make a simple choice,
Or to count out correct change.
Work undone,
And not being able to lift a finger.
Doubting that God cares,
Doubting in my prayers,
Doubting He's even there.
Sitting, staring wild-eyed into space,
Desperately wanting out of the human race.

This unknown writer was in a similar state of mind as the author of Psalm 143. What is described happens – even to a "man after God's own heart."

These passages are a tiny sampling of a large volume expressing David's struggle with his feelings. If David and other psalmists did not deal with depression, they dealt with something quite similar.[20]

## Elijah

Elijah's biography reports great success.

- Elijah declared to Ahab that there would be no dew or rain (1 Kings 17:1). The prophecy was fulfilled.
- Elijah asked a woman to make him a cake with her last oil and meal. Miraculously, God replenished her supply of both, (1 Kings 17:13-16).
- At Elijah's prayer, a dead child was raised to life, (1 Kings 17:18-24).
- Elijah prayed, and fire came from heaven, (1 Kings 18:36).
- When Elijah prayed for rain, God answered, (1 Kings 18:42-46).

Elijah was a remarkable success in a difficult time. The opposition to him and his God was great. Still Elijah persevered. From no angle was there reason for Elijah to feel he had failed.

---

[20] An accompanying book, *Songs for the Dark Place* by Carlton and Norma Coon brings together psalms that are beneficial to read aloud while battling to overcome depression.

But, check on Elijah shortly after two notable miracles:

*But he [Elijah] himself went a day's journey into the wilderness*
*and came and sat down under a juniper tree: and <u>he requested for himself</u>*
*<u>that he might die</u>; and said, It is enough; now, O LORD,*
*take away my life; for I am not better than my fathers,*
**1 Kings 19:4**

Interesting prayer meeting. The man of God praying to die. Many who battle depression have prayed that prayer.

Five verses later, Elijah is shown to be living in a cave. The five verses cover a time period of forty days. Forty days later, Elijah was little better than he had been under the juniper tree. He feels pathetic. Elijah saw himself as a man alone. There are no other prophets faithful to God. Every other person had abandoned both God and Elijah.

Like Job and David, Elijah is using the language of depression. Forty days is a long time to be low. Elijah was not having a blue day. There are symptoms of depression in Elijah's behavior:

- Elijah isolated himself. No one was with him.
- Elijah prayed to die.
- Elijah despaired of his value even though he had been effective.

## God Works With Weakness

Patsy Clairmont's book title, *God Uses Cracked Pots* is correct. God uses weak and wounded people. Peter denied His Lord; Paul could be harsh; Adam and Eve ruined the perfect marriage; Jonah became depressed when an entire heathen city was not burned to a crisp.[21] God was with these – and He was with Job, David, and Elijah.

## The Depressed Christ?

Jesus is the great high priest who can be touched with the feeling of our infirmities (Hebrews 4:15). We easily apply that truth to our physical ailments. Is it necessary for an infirmity to be physical for

---

[21] Wilkerson, David; *Have You Felt Like Giving Up Lately.* (Fleming H. Revell, Grand Rapids, Michigan) P. 113-114.

Jesus to be touched? Much infirmity is mental, emotional, and spiritual.

The same verse (Hebrews 4:15) continues, "Jesus was tempted in like manner as we . . ." On occasion, it is tempting to curl up and quit on life. Is that particular struggle, an infirmity foreign to Jesus?

Matthew 26 records the Passion Week. As Jesus' arrest drew near, Jesus and His closest followers were in The Garden of Gethsemane. Read in any translation, the experience in the Garden of Gethsemane was intense. The Amplified Bible translates Matthew 26:37b,

*[Jesus] began to show grief and distress of mind and was deeply depressed.*

Did Jesus Christ, God manifest in the flesh, struggle with depression? Listen in on His prayer in Gethsemane or the prayer from the cross. "God, why have you forsaken me?" Imagine your best friend asking that exact question. Some would rebuke a believer for asking such a thing. In the Passion Week, Jesus declared His feeling of abandonment. The words He used are words common to those battling depression.

"Jesus, the Depressed" is an unexpected topic. It does not gain significant attention as part of the behavior of Jesus. But, this high priest can be touched with the feeling of all your infirmities. If you experience a Major Depressive Disorder realize that Jesus knows your feelings.

# Chapter 5
# Impacting People Have Battled Depression

Many significant people have endured depression. Perhaps depression is part of a process that turns human carbon into a human diamond? The tree that has to withstand the fiercest storms becomes deep-rooted and strong. The fight to overcome depression may well prove to be the very agent that drives us to God and makes us strong.[22] Such an observation does not make depression any easier.

## C. H. Spurgeon

Charles Haddon Spurgeon is often referenced. It is with good reason. He pastored London's Metropolitan Tabernacle. It was a church of thousands. Spurgeon authored over two hundred books, including the masterful *Treasury of David*. In his day, Spurgeon was respected, loved, and emulated. Most concepts in Spurgeon's book, *Lectures to My Students* would fit any modern curriculum for training preachers.

We would assume Spurgeon was satisfied with life. Surely Spurgeon felt energetic and fulfilled. The facts are different. For no visible reason, Spurgeon carried a heavy burden of depression throughout his life.

One Sunday, C.H. Spurgeon shocked 5,000 listeners when he said, "I am the subject of depressions of spirit so fearful that I hope none of you ever gets to such extremes of wretchedness as I go to."

On another occasion Spurgeon recounted, "I could weep by the hour like a child, and yet I knew not what I wept for."[23]

Richard Day is a Spurgeon biographer. He wrote, "There was one aspect of Spurgeon's life, glossed over by most of his biographers, which we must now view with utter frankness: he was frequently in the grip of terrific depression."

---

[22] Sanders, *Facing Loneliness*, P. 157.

[23] Amundson, Darrel; *The Anguish and Agonies of Charles Spurgeon, Christian History 10* (Christian History Institute, 1991) p. 64.

Spurgeon was often physically ill. He would be in bed for weeks at a time. Sickness was so common that Spurgeon told the leaders of his church they ought to replace him.

Regular bouts of such illness is not uncommon for those who battle depression. Depression not only affects mind and emotions, it also weakens the physical body.

Spurgeon, like all of us, had his doubts, anxieties, and deep struggles with emotion. Success, popularity, accomplishment nor fame improved Charles Spurgeon's emotional condition.

## J. B. Phillips

The J.B. Phillips translation of the New Testament is commonly used as a reference. Phillip's excellent little book, *Your God is Too Small* incites faith.

Often overlooked is Phillips' experience with depression. He was hospitalized for depression on more than one occasion. In Phillips autobiography, *The Price of Success*, he wrote:

I know now, but had no idea then, that this was the first inkling of . . . depression, a condition that was to be with me for several years. After a few months, . . . I found the mental pain more than I felt I could bear, and I went as a voluntary patient to a psychiatric ward.

My reason for writing about this is that it may help someone else who is depressed and in mental pain. It may help simply to know that one whom the world would regard as successful and whose worldly needs are comfortably met can still enter this particular hell, and have to endure it for quite a long time.[24]

## Abraham Lincoln

In 1841, several years before becoming President of the United States, Abraham Lincoln wrote to a friend, "I am now the most miserable man living. If what I feel were equally distributed to the whole human family, there would not be one cheerful face on earth.

---

[24] Phillips, J.B., *The Price of Success*, (Shaw Books; Wheaton, IL; 1984.) P. 197.

Whether I shall ever feel better, I cannot tell. I forebode I shall not. To remain as I am is impossible. I must die or be better, it appears to me."

On another occasion Lincoln, wrote to his wife, "I have gotten my spirits so low that I feel I would rather be any place in the world than here. I really cannot endure the thought of staying here another two weeks."

Lincoln understood the danger a depressed person faced. During one bout with depression, Lincoln's friends kept knives and razors away from him. The future president did not carry a pocketknife for months, apparently fearful of his suicidal tendencies.

### The Known but Unidentified

God specializes in using flawed instruments. Those who have great gifting may also have great struggles. The five-talent man can also have five liabilities. Four people of my church culture come to mind. If their names were reported, hundreds of thousands of people would know them. Most people would be shocked to know the darkness through which these notable people walked.

One, was a man God used as an apostle, prophet, pastor, teacher and evangelist. His ministry was remarkable. There were miracles of healing and deliverance. His experience of companying with angels and contesting with the demonic were real. There was no self-aggrandizement or posturing about him. He never told a story to make himself look good.

The man was accessible to young preachers. When I called, he was always available. Our conversation would usually range far afield from the reason for my call. This man of unique calling and anointing had time for me when my prospects were quite dim.

The less-known reality is the man's struggle with depression. The phrase "nervous breakdown" was applied to at least one season of his life. The man of great prayer, faith, integrity, and common sense would enter dark seasons. Each day would be a challenge. To put the severity of his depression into perspective, he was diagnosed with what was then called clinical depression, and took medicine to counter the impact of depression.

A second woman has been a person of impact since her teenage years. Her speaking, books, and influence have helped hundreds of thousands of people. In the middle season and later years of life, she has walked through the swamp of despair. At times, she has been a "shell of normal." There is little external reason for her to be depressed. Yet, she is. This lady of prayer and great accomplishment was diagnosed with Major Depressive Disorder and on occasion, took medicine to combat the illness.

The third person is an author and speaker of renown. He has spoken at hundreds of ministerial training and leadership events. His books have sold far more than mine. This fellow has battled with depression to the point of having been suicidal. On at least one occasion, he was temporarily institutionalized to protect his well-being. Medication and counsel has helped him endure.

A fourth comes to mind. The fellow preached great meetings. Thousands were converted. These were seasons of great enthusiasm and energy. As was true for Spurgeon and J.B. Phillips, there were other seasons. His closest confidantes and friends speak of him being so depressed as not to be able to function normally.

Has God chosen to make use of people with the greatest flaws? Perhaps. It is more likely that depression, which we so want to avoid, is part of what shapes the person to fit God's purpose.

*Success, accomplishment, talent, and fame*
*are no insurance*
*against the struggle of depression.*

In college days, many of us had a bit of contact with John Milton and *Paradise Lost*. Milton wrote, "The mind in its own place, and of itself / Can make a Heaven of Hell, a Hell of Heaven." Milton's words aptly describe depression. Depression can make a "hell of heaven."

Biographers report that many people of fame and accomplishment battled depression. The list includes musicians Beethoven, Tchaikovsky, and John Lennon. Artists Georgia O'Keefe and Vincent Van Gogh are on the list. As are Mark Twain, Virginia Woolf, and

Earnest Hemingway. Hall of Fame athlete Terry Bradshaw speaks and writes of his depression.

People of impact in music, art, literature, politics, athletics and religion have battled depression. Depression must not be shunted aside as laziness or a character flaw. Many successful people have survived depression accomplishing great things in spite of having battled this particular dragon.

# Chapter 6
# Why Is Depression Such a No-No?

There are many reasons to avoid the discussion about depression.
Three reasons are commonly mentioned.

<u>Depression is linked to psychiatry and psychology.</u>

Both fields draw skepticism. These are comparatively new areas of
research. Some skepticism is warranted. It results from psychologists
or psychiatrists making deductions inconsistent with the Bible. Those
deductions are not correct. But all deductions of mental health
professionals and counselors are not incorrect. Every mental health
professional is not opposed to the work of the Lord Jesus Christ.

Sigmund Freud became somewhat bizarre late in life. Freud's
negative attitude toward religion in general is well documented.
Many of his observations are far-fetched. But Freud's simple
definition of psychological health seems accurate. He said
psychological health was: being able to love and work.[25]

In this case Freud's definition is beneficial and parallels principles
expressed in the Bible. Should we throw the good out with the bad?

<u>"Victory in Jesus" and depression seem to be inconsistent terms.</u>

The attitude tends to be, "Testify of yesterday's depression, of
what you went through six months ago. Now that you are through it,
we will celebrate your victory. But don't tell us about your
depression while you are going through it."

We are not sure of how to respond to the person who is depressed
- now! The "name it and claim it" crowd would have you imagine
life as a magic carpet ride to heaven. They have it wrong. Christians
will have "victory in Jesus" even as they deal with both physical
illness and emotional struggles.

---

[25] Storr, Anthony. *Churchill's Black Dog, Kafka's Mice and Other Phenomena of
the Human Brain* (Ballantine Books, New York, 1990) P. vii.

## Over-spiritualizing life

Some imagine the presence of depression means a person has sinned. If sin is always the reason for depression, then the solution is simple. If a depressed person only repents and makes restitution, the depression goes away. If some other malady is the cause then repentance will not correct the difficulty.

Over-spiritualizing leaves us with four mistaken ideas about depression:

1. Depression is always the result of sin.
2. Depression is caused by a lack of faith in God.
3. Depression means God's face is turned against us.
4. Being healed from depression is a spiritual exercise accomplished by prayer and other spiritual disciplines.[26]

While depression can be the result of sin, this is not always the case. Such incorrect assumptions make addressing the experience of depression difficult. A depressed person may do as they are told. They search their heart and repent of known (and unknown) sin but their despair does not leave.

At a conference, I was talking about the work I was doing for, *Light in a Dark Place.* Another author, a quite capable lady, listened to my plan to write about "understanding and overcoming depression." She interjected, "Depression, ah, I don't believe in that."

Unfortunately, her attitude is far too prevalent. It is difficult enough to encounter depression, without the Christian body acting as though depression is a figment of the imagination, or is always the result of sin.

Being willing to accept depression as something real is a first step toward getting help or being a helper. Someone battling depression is already struggling. He knows what the idealized Christian life is. Like any other Christian, his ambition is joy, peace, victory, overcoming, and rejoicing.

---

[26] Hart, Archibald, *Counseling the Depressed*, Volume 5 from *Resources for Christian Counseling* (Waco, Texas; Word Books, 1987). Gary Collins, General Editor. P. 25-29.

Yet that ideal is not happening. The challenge is worse if those around him are unable to allow the person to be honest about the challenge.

# Chapter 7
# Movie Sets and False Fronts

Movies portray the unreal. On film, an old town is seen. However, on the movie set, the old town is usually only the front walls. It has a certain look for the camera, but no substance.

A depressed person's smile is a movie set. It looks good, but the smile is skin deep. In public, a depressed person displays a thin veneer of being "ok."

In the old West, some business owners built their store with what appeared to be a second floor. The look didn't fool many people. The building only appeared to have a second floor if you stood directly in front of it. From any other angle, the false front was obvious.

The goal of "false front" architecture was to project an image of success. The business owner may not have invested much money in the building. It may have been poorly built. The building might only be temporary.[27] But the "false front" presented the sense that things were good.

High performing individuals who have Major Depressive Disorder may use their energy to do well in public. No co-worker of fellow worshipper would imagine them to be depressed. At home, life is quite different. Several weeks' worth of dishes are unwashed, clothes have not been put away, bills are not paid and the home is in complete disarray. A co-worker or fellow-worshipper does not see the mental pain and exhaustion. There is much "false front" living.

Don't misunderstand. A depressed person is not being hypocritical or putting on a show. There is not enough energy to put on a show. The depressed person is using all available energy to appear normal.

How would it be received, if a "pillar of the church" offered a sincere prayer request saying, "I've been asking the Lord to let me die? Would you join me in my prayer?" People would be askance at his request. Instead, the man will muster the strength to act normal.

---

[27] https://en.wikipedia.org/wiki/Western_false_front_architecture (read January 5, 2018).

Even while acting normal in public, in private, that "pillar of the church" may well have joined Job and Elijah in asking the Lord Jesus to let him die. This "false front" is the depressed person's best effort to survive with public credibility intact.

While carrying the shadow that sits heavy, a person retreats from life as much as possible. But, all of life cannot be avoided. A job, family responsibilities, and church-life continue. Since the depressed person cannot resign from life, they try to present themselves as normal. But just behind the false front, there is sadness, terror, and loneliness.

## Just Getting By

The best option for the person who is depressed seems to be to muster lagging energy and carry on the social pleasantries. Those who casually interact with someone depressed will not know of the struggle. Each *normal* encounter expends some of the little energy available.

"Hiding" the depression drains physical, mental, spiritual and emotional reserves and worsens the depression. At the same time, the inner man is, as one counselor put it, "bleeding out." It is all part of the struggle to stay upright. David understood such struggles. He wrote,

> *...my steps had well nigh slipped.*
> **Psalms 73:2**

The struggle to keep the public false front in place is one reason depressed people withdraw. The fewer people they see, the less energy need be expended on, "Being fine."

This week, people with these traits will sit in churches all over the world. Those people long for understanding and hope for help.

# Section II
# The Substance Behind The Shadow

From the cradle to the grave, man never does a
single thing
which has any first and foremost objective,
save one:
to secure peace of mind and spiritual comfort for
himself.
**Mark Twain**

# Chapter 8
# Diagnosing Depression

A diagnosis of Major Depressive Disorder is given when at least five of the following nine symptoms have been present for two weeks or longer. Further, these symptoms must be significantly interfering with a person having the ability to function in social settings:

- Persistent sadness, unhappiness, or irritability.
- Lethargy or fatigue.
- Loss of interest in previously enjoyable activities.
- A sudden change in appetite.
- The disruption of normal sleep patterns.
- Feeling guilty or worthless.
- Moving about more slowly and sluggishly, or feeling restless and needing to move all the time.
- Difficulty thinking or concentrating.
- Recurrent thoughts of suicide or death.[28]

These symptoms are clearly more than a "blue day."

## Depression is Serious

Depressed people tend to become extremely introspective in a self-derogatory way. The mental conversation is one-sided. It is all negative. Past mistakes, self-blame, and real or imagined failures are the sum of the inner talk.[29]

What brings on MDD? Many things initiate depression:

- Childbirth may result in postpartum depression.
- Advancing age
- Adolescence
- Sexual, mental, physical, or emotional abuse.
- Addiction, whether to alcohol, drugs, food, success, or sex.

---

[28] Biebel and Koenig P. 45
[29] Minirth, Hawkins, Meier, *Happy Holidays* P. 28

- Ongoing sin.
- None of the above! Sometimes depression comes to people who cannot find a root cause.

It is difficult for a non-diabetic to comprehend the challenges of someone with diabetes. In a similar way, few people who have not experienced depression can understand what happens during a season of depression.

Depressed people are exhausted and overwhelmed much of the time. MDD is an enormous weight. They would do almost anything to be rid of the weight. They are like Christian in *Pilgrim's Progress,* who in one portion of the book, experiences despair. Depression can transform what would be a beautiful and pleasant time of life into a prison having no visible bars.

Like many illnesses, depression is complicated. People with depression may have abnormally low levels of certain brain chemicals, and slowed cellular activity in areas of the brain that control mood, appetite, sleep, and other functions.[30]

The items just cited from Mayo Clinic's research does not include spiritual matters. Yet, the spiritual aspect cannot be ignored while considering depression. Sin and the spiritual condition can certainly affect a person's emotions.

---

[30] Kramlinger, Keith M.D. P.76

# Chapter 9
# What is A Depressed Brain?

The science presented in this chapter is elementary at best. In the process of time, researchers may make discoveries that render things written here inaccurate. Aspects of my explanation are poorly presented. This chapter was presented to, and discussed with several people who have doctorates in the mental health field. I take responsibility for any lacking found here.

This chapter nor any other should be a deciding factor regarding your health. Don't self-diagnose. Visit your Medical Doctor for a thorough review of any condition

There is likely more unknown about the human mind than that which is known. It is sufficient to say, the human brain is an amazing representation of the creativity of the Lord Jesus Christ.

One area of the brain is known as the limbic system. Together with some other parts of the brain, the limbic system allows us to experience feelings of joy, happiness, wonder, and awe. The limbic system is the part of the brain most affected by depression.[31]

In our body, particular substances are needed for health. Without insulin, your body is in trouble. A healthy pancreas secretes the proper amount of insulin to keep a body well. When the pancreas does not do this, a person is soon ill.

The person whose pancreas is not correctly functioning may be wealthy and have wonderful relationships. He may be a great preacher or singer. Regardless of possessions, position, or relationships, the person will not be healthy. The other positive experiences of life will not take the place of a person's pancreas not functioning correctly.

---

[31] Biebel and Koenig p. 35-36

In a similar way, our brain needs particular substances to function correctly. One path to Major Depressive Disorder is biochemical. A biochemical is a biologically generated chemical. When the body is operating as it should, glands and specific cells in the body naturally create these biochemicals. Again, think of insulin's effect on health.

The trigger toward depression may be a physical accident, grief, a surgery, anxiety, guilt regarding sin, or some other reason. The starting point is certainly important. But if depression is the outcome, regardless of what triggered it, the depression needs to be addressed. Recognizing depression as abnormal is the first step toward getting help. A person diagnosed with a Major Depressive Disorder is not healthy, just as a person with diabetes is not healthy.

The biochemicals mentioned earlier operate in the brain by the use of neurotransmitters. A neurotransmitter is a chemical that is released at the end of a nerve fiber. This release happens at the arrival of a nerve impulse. The neurotransmitter helps bridge the gap between cells as it causes the transfer of the impulse to another nerve fiber, a muscle fiber, or some other structure of the human body.

When everything works as it should, the biochemical is more or less *fired* from a nerve ending on one cell into a neuro-receptor on another cell. Envision, the biochemical being *fired* like a cannon shooting a cannonball. As the neurotransmitter *fires*, the needed biochemical moves from one cell to another.

The neuro-receptor that has received the biochemical then distributes the biochemical to where it needs to go. Emotional and mental health require the correct amount of such biochemicals to stabilize mood.

My man-on-the-street description of depression is something like this: Your body doesn't produce enough of the needed biochemical. Thus,, the amount and number of times the neurotransmitter *fires the cannon* is decreased. The neuro-receptor in a neighboring cell has nothing to send further into your limbic system.

People with MDD may well be experiencing a degree of biochemical depletion. Depression coming from a lack of the needed neurotransmitters usually exhibits itself in one or both of the following:

56

1. Absence of pleasure - nothing brightens the person's mood. Their sense of humor is gone. There is little enjoyment of anything. You cannot cheer them up. It frustrates a depressed person when someone tries to cheer them.
2. An unresponsive mood - a normal person reacts to the group around them. A biochemically depressed person remains impassive and oblivious. They may try to, "Put it on," as to seem to be engaged in what is happening. This is a "false front." A depressed person knows a certain level of engagement is expected. They do their best to accomplish this engagement.

The human brain has about 14 billion cells. These 14 billion cells have an unlimited number of combinations of nerve endings. At the intersection of each nerve ending with other nerve endings, there is a place where the two cells almost touch. The interaction between the two cells happens via the neurotransmitters mentioned earlier.

The neurotransmitter provides a connection between the two nerve endings.[32] Where there is an inadequate interaction, because of too few neurotransmitters, our brain cells are impaired. The cells do not communicate with each other at a normal pace.

The brain needs millions such neurotransmitters. When a person is depressed for two weeks or more, research has indicated that one or more of the neurotransmitters, is not available in adequate numbers.

Serotonin is the primary biochemical affecting our mood. Increasing serotonin in the body and brain so that enough of it moves from a transmitter to receptor is one key to decreasing or eliminating the symptoms of depression.

If biochemical issues are involved, depression is as much a physical disease as diabetes, tuberculosis, or gout. A pathological illness is taking place.[33] If a victim to diabetes, tuberculosis, or gout does not receive the right treatment, the person will suffer. A person

---

[32] Mallory, James D. and Hefley, James C. *Untwisted Living*. (Wheaton, Illinois; Victor Books, 1982.) P. 64

[33] Maughon, p. 16

whose depression is not addressed will also suffer. Should we not then give depression the same significance as gout or a migraine headache?

# Chapter 10
# Caution: Bridge Out

When Hurricane Katrina made landfall in August of 2005, I was leading a mission's effort for a major religious organization. David Tipton, a Mississippian involved in the recovery, took me on a tour of Mississippi and Louisiana. As we traveled west on Interstate 10, there were several places where Katrina's storm surge had destroyed entire sections of the causeway. On either side of the missing span, all was well. But where a section of the bridge was gone travel was reduce to two lanes.

The missing sections of bridges slowed travel. On a normal afternoon, with all lanes open, traffic might have proceeded at 70 miles per hour. With bridges washed out, traffic moved at closer to 30 miles per hour.

In Major Disruptive Disorder, the neurotransmitters - bridges for the human brain, are not adequately available. The communication between cells of the brain is not occurring at the normal pace. In depression, nerve impulses that drive thought, behavior, responses, and feelings slow down. Mental and emotional traffic may come to a near halt.

Depression not only affects the emotions. Depression slows everything:

- The person may physically move slower than usual.
- Mental processes are not as quick as normal.
- Conversation is labored.

This is frustrating. Family members become impatient. The depressed person is frustrated. He is also embarrassed that he can't hold a normal conversation.

When depressed, a person who normally responds quickly to a question, will deliberate for a seemingly everlasting length of time. The question was heard. But suddenly choosing between chocolate, vanilla, or strawberry ice-cream is hard. A depressed person is not being rude. The normal response won't come.

From personal experience, someone may ask a question. The response is there. Just there – within reach. But capturing the thought is like catching dandelion seed blown by the wind. The answer can be seen. It is just before me, but mysterious and incomplete.

Eventually, the elusive thought is captured. Now, the answer is front and center. The answer is in the mind. But the problem isn't resolved. Words are needed to express the answer. The correct words must be gathered, and sentences put together. The answer is there, but the words won't come together. The phrases won't flow. Neurotransmitters are not providing the bridge between nerve endings. Mental traffic is moving slowly.

Depressed people, who are normally coherent and highly capable, may be thought stupid. Worse, the depressed person feels stupid. MDD affects more than the emotions.

## Repairing the Bridges

After Hurricane Katrina, it took several months to repair Interstate 10. Short-term solutions included building temporary bridges over some destroyed spans. All this time, the pace of traffic was slow.

Similarly, unless there is instantaneous healing, recovery from depression takes time. The depressed person and those around him will need patience.

## Keep Moving

Depressed people are tempted to find an "off-ramp" and park their life. Since nothing comes easy, "I quit." This is the wrong response. Slow movement is better than no movement. In the aftermath of Katrina, the traffic moved slowly; but it moved.

When a person's "norm" is to move through life at a quick pace it is frustrating to be slowed by what feels like ineptness. However, you never get past the "bridge out" part of life if you stop. On that fall day in southern Mississippi, David Tipton and I kept travelling. It was a slow go. In time, we arrived at our destination. A slow go is better than "no go."

# Chapter 11
# Imbalance

Depression can result from unbalanced living. A person who over-engages one part of life and leaves other important things behind is at risk on several fronts. One potential outcome is depression.

A man who pours himself into a career and misses the wonder of being a parent is such a person. In later years, the man may realize his folly. It is often too late to undo the damage done to his family. The realization of his poor choices can become a trigger for depression.

Imbalance in the pursuit of success, wealth, pleasure, hobbies, sports, or any other interest can result in depression.

## Unrealistic Expectations

Imbalance may occur as a result of having unrealistic expectations about life. An imperfect person marries the "perfect spouse," and soon discovers their spouse's flaws. The person went into the marriage with unrealistic expectations.

For over a decade, much of my work was with church planters. Some failed to plant a church because of starting with unrealistic expectations. Unrealistic expectations lead to disappointment. Disappointment becomes discouragement which leads to a sense of failure. At times, the sense of failure led to a battle of deep depression for the church planter. The journey into depression began with unrealistic expectations.

In Jesus' teaching of life's challenges, He said,

> ...*In this world, you will have trouble...*
> **John 16:33 (NIV)**

No person is strong enough, has enough education, or is wise enough to avoid trouble. If you write an autobiography, "trouble" will be in every chapter. Don't be surprised. Expect it! Then, you will not live with unrealistic expectations.

Scott Peck's book, *The Road Less Traveled*, emphasizes that for almost everyone, life is hard most of the time. Peck sees the root of much mental illness as an attempt to avoid the hardness of life by any means necessary. Trying to avoid life's difficulty is certainly the source of much addiction. Having unrealistic expectations keeps you off-balance.

## The Importance of Balance

Some time back, my wife, Norma, and I worked with a personal trainer. Our goal was to be more "fit for the fight." Our trainer, Eddie's initial evaluation included a test to determine our physical balance.

I asked Eddie what balance had to do with fitness. He explained that people with poor balance are more likely to fall. Also, certain exercises could not be done if we did not have good balance. In the initial test, Norma had the better physical balance. In time, the workouts improved my balance.

The better a person's physical balance, the more capable they are of surviving a misstep. The better a person's emotional balance, the less likely they are of being overwhelmed when depression comes.

# Chapter 12
# Depression's Cost

It is hard to assess *what might have been*. Some of depression's costs are not easily detected. Suffice it to say that depression is expensive to an individual, to families, and to society.

Andrew Solomon in *The Noonday Demon* wrote, "Depression claims more years than war, cancer, and AIDS put together. Other illnesses, from alcoholism to heart disease, mask depression when it is depression that caused them: if one considers that, depression may be the biggest killer on the earth."[34]

The Global Burden of Disease (GBD) assesses mortality and disability from major diseases, injuries, and risk factors. In 2000, The GBD report showed depression as the fourth leading cause of disability worldwide. Depression was the second leading cause of disability for people aged 15-44. The same GBD study predicted that by 2020, depression would be the second leading cause of disability in the world, second only to heart disease.[35]

## What Might Have Been

A sweet elder read my candid article about depression in a magazine. Her husband had been an influential executive in his particular organization. Prompted by my article, she told my wife of her husband's struggle with depression.

At times, her husband would be immobilized by depression. The man accomplished many positive things. The question remains: what might have been accomplished if the depression had been addressed? What books might he have written? What other initiatives might he have successfully completed?

---

[34] Solomon, Andrew; *The Noonday Demon*, (New York, Simon and Schuster, 2002) p. 25

[35] Murray C., Lopez A., *The Global Burden of Disease: A Comprehensive Assessment of Mortality and Disability from Disease, Injuries and Risk Factors in 1990 and Projected to 2020*, Volume 1 (Geneva: World Health Organization, 2000)

The answers elude us. When a gifted person who battles depression looks at life they wonder *what might have been*. Such thoughts only add weight to the shadow that sits heavy.

Disability manifests itself in:

- An inability to maintain relationships with family or friends.
- Not fulfilling a person's job requirements.
- Being unable to relax and enjoy recreation or vacation.

Depression can be more difficult for Christians because the pain they feel is accompanied by guilt that they cannot be who they want to be.

### The Broken Component/the Affected Whole

Depression disturbs the emotions. It also impacts systems that would otherwise work correctly.

The result is a bit like a malfunctioning computer. I'm writing on a six-year-old computer. My computer is a wonderful invention. It multiplies my productivity.

My computer functions as a whole, but it is actually made up of many components. If there is a problem with any component, the machine is slowed or stopped. The difficulty could be any number of things:

- The battery no longer providing power.
- A malfunction with the motherboard.
- The display screen going dark.
- Typing on the keyboard, anticipating an output in my language, but instead seeing Swahili.

A component not working correctly affects the entire computer. Why? The components of the computer are inter-connected; dependent on each other. A failure in any component affects the entire computer.

Something similar is true of the human mind, body, spirit, and emotions. The mind is a component of God's wonderful creation known as the human body. Everything in a person's life can be wonderful, but if one component malfunctions, it affects the whole.

When depression takes hold, it affects the whole man - body, soul, mind, and spirit.

Further consider the computer. If the keyboard is faulty or the screen no longer works, the data on the computer's hard drive is not lost. The information that had been input into the computer remains, though it is currently inaccessible. The *whole* of the computer's capabilities have been affected by the breakdown of a single component.

Depression is not just mental or emotional. Depression impacts everything. When depression hits, people can seem *mentally slow, suddenly stupid,* or *anti-social.*

None of this is true. The depressed person is still talented; and their IQ and social skills have not disappeared. Instead, those capabilities cannot currently be accessed.

A depressed person knows the love of God exists; remembers that mercy is new every day; and recalls that God's mercy endures forever. Yet, the depressed person cannot grasp any of that love and mercy in a functional way.

This is where it becomes crucial for the church body to have a correct response. Here are some suggestions:

- Stand alongside and be supportive. Don't indict or criticize.
- A message to someone you sense to be struggling helps.
- Your hand-written note will likely come at the right time.
- Don't push your way in. Depression takes away the reserves needed for social interaction.

The struggle is intense. Satan would like to turn depression into permanent spiritual defeat. Depression has caused myriads of people to completely backslide. Satan wants a depressed person to reach a place where they imagine, "God is non-existent, and the grave is my goal."

While you are broken and hurting with depression, satan wants to convince you that the data is corrupt. He is wrong! Never forget, satan is a lier and the father of lies. The wonderful thing God created when He made you is still there. In time, you will overcome.

# Chapter 13
# Not in Control

A terrible aspect of depression is the sense of having lost control of life. Life has become a maze with no exit. While depressed a person asks themselves, "What if I never come out of this?" The question is pertinent, because in depression there is no clear path out.

To be in prison without bars, yet a prison from which there seems to be no release describes depression. The sense of "not having control" is the substance behind their shadow.

Lack of control has been proven to affect mice. A university researcher's experiments with mice repeatedly left one seeming withdrawn, dejected, and lacking in energy. The other mouse acted normal. What was the experiment?

Two mice were placed in a cage with a wheel on one wall. The mice were separated by a clear barrier. The two mice could see each other. The mouse on the left side of the cage was given control of the wheel.

The goal was to get the mouse on the left trained to turn the wheel. While the wheel turned, all was well – there was peace - for both mice.

When the wheel stopped turning, both mice received a small electric shock. The mouse on the right was being shocked for something over which it had no control. After repeating the experiment several times, these observations were made:

- The mouse with control of the wheel behaved normally. When the wheel stopped turning, and he was shocked, the small shock was accepted without lasting impact. The mouse went on with life. To be shocked or not was within that mouse's control.
- The mouse that had no control over the outcome became dejected and withdrawn. He was not shocked any harder than the mouse on the other side of the cage. But the second mouse had no control as to whether or not a shock was coming.

The mouse shocked through no fault of its own showed classic symptoms of depression. It stopped eating; became listless and had no interest in its surroundings. When something usually of great interest to mice, like cheese or peanut-butter, was put in his cage, the depressed mouse ignored it.

## When the Mice are Men

Any person perpetually living in a prison called "hopeless" is a candidate for depression. The effect of a season of hopelessness has a residual impact. It may not go away.

Interestingly, when the researcher moved the "depressed" mouse to the side of the cage where he now had control, the mouse never recovered from his earlier experience. His time of living without control had taken away the verve and vitality for life. Though things were now better, the mouse had already given up. Depression had become a new *norm* even though the circumstances had changed.[36]

Stress, like that experienced by the unfortunate mice, can be the basis of depression. At work, not being in control is common. The boss tells us what to do. Major upheavals are often beyond our control: changing jobs or marital distresses are stressful.

Minor irritations like broken office equipment is also stressful. One study showed that daily hassles are more likely to have a greater effect on an individual's moods and attitudes than the major misfortunes of life.[37]

## Live in this Moment

A solution to the challenge of not being in control can be to live in the moment. Accept what you cannot change. The past, and other people's behavior are common sources of lasting pain. Neither of these are matters we can control.

The pains are real, but depression need not be the flavor of life. A depressed person will help themselves by setting a simple goal. The

---

[36] Gold, Mark S.; *The Good News About Depression*; (New York: Bantam Books, 1995). P. 170.

[37] Thomas, Marian.; *A New Attitude*; (National Press Publications; Shawnee Mission, Kansas, 1991) P. 77.

goal must be something in their control. Even a small goal can cause a person to look to the future. Accomplishing a small goal gives a mental and emotional "win."

The past is sealed and settled. Yesterday can be addressed and responded to with perspective, counsel, and forgiveness. But yesterday cannot be undone. If there are things in the past to address, then seek help getting it done. Don't let yesterday determine your future. Yesterday's experiences are a report, while tomorrow is a blank page.

## Childhood Trauma

Many battle depression because of a past over which they had no control. Childhood trauma has longterm effects. Observing domestic violence as well as mental, psychologial, verbal, sexual, and physical abuse are "the shocks" over which a child has no control.

Adults who experienced this sort of childhood may have little energy for life. Without them even realizing it, depression is a constant companion. Depression is the norm. They have known nothing else.

## Post Traumatic Stress Disorder (PTSD)

Many veterans returning from military combat bring home the sandy grit of depression. The grit hides in horrors experienced. Horrors of which they can seldom speak. PTSD not only affects those in the military; it also impacts "first responders."

People in such circumstances have little control over what comes at them. The ugly underbelly of life is not only seen; the person also becomes a participant.

Afterward, an emotional undertow sets in. A constant drag pulls the person down. Faces and situations flash before their eyes. In the memory of the trauma, yet again, the first responder or warrior has no control.

Depression becomes a constant undesirable traveling companion. A companion some people come to know all too well.

Everyone has parts of life over which there is no control. A pastor, who watches good people self-destruct, in spite of repeated warnings, can become depressed. Dentists and those who work in a hospital Emergency Room are prime candidates for depression. In both settings, the health care provider seldom sees a patient who is not in pain.

In places where we have no choice but to toil on, the shadow sits heavy. Depression is not something tangible a person can reach out and grasp.

Pastor Dewayne Butler is a medical professional who served as a coroner in Louisiana. He worked closely with first responders and has seen the impact PTSD has on its victims. He said, "People who suffer from PTSD have been exposed to situations that are not close to normal. Those in the military experience the same. PTSD brings them a sense of loneliness and depression."

## When Depression is "Just" Accepted

Some surrender to depression by accepting its symptoms as difficult, but endurable. However, such surrender is not acceptable. The problem: emotions are now driving a person's behavior. The person who accepts depression as their permanent normal may stop attending church, quit work, or stay up all night to avoid human interaction.

Accepted hopelessness is a tragedy. The words over the French prison gate, "Abandon hope all ye who enter here," becomes a mantra to a person who just accepts their depression. When a person stops battling, their depression becomes a vast sea that has no shores.

Actually, few depressed people are truly without hope. The next section will introduce strategies for fighting back.

# Section III
# Strategies to Survive Depression

*We are ultimately responsible for our own self-care,
and we can do a great deal to help ourselves
break free from depression.*
**David Hazard**

*The good news is that depression is treatable.*
**Medicine in the Public Interest**

# Chapter 14
# Decide to Fight It

Surviving and finding God in the dark place isn't glitzy, quick, or easy. I wish that a *Daniel's Fast*, memorizing the books of the Bible, or being able to quote the book of Proverbs was a solution. They aren't.

There are some things that can help overcome depression. For any of them to work, you must determine to fight back. Fighting depression is not easy. The first problem is that energy to fight is lacking.

The Lord Jesus Christ and His Bible are solution-oriented. The Bible instructs that there are times to *rebuke*. It also says to *exhort*, (2 Timothy 4:2). To *exhort* includes the idea of coaching someone. This section of the book will coach you on actions you can take to battle the darkness.

Florence Littauer wrote, "Many books I've read on depression have been:

Too dull or too deep.
Too serious or too sad.
Too heavy or too hopeless.

They have shown:
Gloom with no glamour
Life with no lilt,
Sorrow with no solution."

*Light in a Dark Place* is not the sort of book Littauer described. Depressed people need workable solutions that do not require the ability to run a marathon or participate in a debate on Scientology.

## The Suggestions from the Unknowing

Most suggestions from those who have never dealt with depression are clumsy at best. Well-meaning people advise, "Pray your way through it." That is one of the better suggestions. Some suggestions are goofy. Martha Maughon battled depression. In an

73

attempt to help and encourage her, one of Martha's acquaintances suggested, "Go out and buy yourself a new hat."[38]

A person giving such advice is clueless. It is like someone giving travel directions to a place they have never been. A person who has traveled into and out of depression is a better travel guide.

Frank Minirth and Paul Meir wrote, *Happiness is a Choice*. They declare that while we have little control over our emotions, our behavior is under the control of our will. You may not be able to control depression. But, you can be responsible for your reactions. Help can only come if we accept responsibility for ourselves.

Most of the coming suggestions are simple. All of them will require some effort. Most recommendations require a change of behavior. If you are not willing to make a try at changing your behavior, then no book or counselor can help.

Are you open to behaviors that may help deal with depression, even if the benefit you receive is marginal?

- Are you willing to have a regular time to go to bed and to awaken each morning?
- Will you do some moderate, but consistent exercise?
- Are you willing to strip life to the bare essentials?
- Are you willing to read material to better understand depression and how to overcome it?
- Are you willing to adjust your diet? *Sugar Blues* by William Dufty is an enlightening and worthy read.

Little progress is made in overcoming depression if we blame past experiences or our genetic makeup. Such things may have positioned us to more easily fall into depression, but we can permit ourselves no excuse.

Victors over Major Depressive Disorder have experienced terrible things.

- Sexual abuse by a parent or religious leader.
- Medical care that unintentionally encourages staying in the pit of despair.

---

[38] Maughon, P. 72.

- Rape and sexual molestation.
- Permanent disfigurement by fire.
- Involvement with a homosexual lifestyle.
- A childhood surrounded by drugs and alcohol.
- Aborting an unborn child.
- Addiction to a lazy, sedentary life funded by taxpayers.
- Long-term chemical imbalance.
- Mental abuse.
- Imprisonment.
- Drug abuse.
- And so many others.

Those who became victors battled their depression. Depression had them firmly in its grasp. But winners never stop fighting. Will you decide to fight?

Action is necessary to overcome depression. Assessing and perhaps revitalizing your spiritual life is always a good first step. Other steps will likely be necessary. Minirth and Meier include the idea that a depressed person's need to find ways to minister to other people.[39] Living on an island named "self" is a path to certain defeat.

As we enter this section, ask yourself the following:

1. Do you realize you have a problem?
2. Do you want help or have you decided to permanently accept defeat?
3. Are you drowning in self-pity?[40]

Several things have helped me survive. And no, buying a new hat was not one of them. Martha Maughon did not get a new hat either. It would not have worked for us. What a new hat won't do, some other things may be able to do.

---

[39] Minirth, Frank, Meier Paul, Meier Richard, Hawkins Don; *The Healthy Christian Life* (Grand Rapids, Michigan, Baker Book House, 1988) P. 108.

[40] Littauer, Florence, *Blow Away the Black Clouds; A Woman's Answer to Depression*, (Eugene, OR; Harvest House Publishers; 1986) P. 46-48

# Chapter 15
# Simplify Your Life

Remember the mouse who became depressed? The poor creature could not change the rules of the experiment.

You are not that mouse. You have options. Those options may be limited, but you have options.

Depression can happen when people make requests and we cannot respond appropriately.[41] We follow the trail of least resistance by saying, "Yes," to everything asked.

Some indications that a depressed person needs to simplify:

- You are exhausted and someone seeks help with a project. The person asking could do it themselves or they could ask another person. Will you do the task anyway?
- You have done your part on a project. A coworker who has not done her part now asks for your help at the last instant. Will you rescue her?
- Someone who is not good with money asks you for a loan or gift. You know he has wasted money or has not worked a job when he could. Will you give him the money anyway?

A depressed person is likely to say, "Yes," though they know they should not. A depressed person has little energy and tends to "cave" in. With the overwhelming pace of life, when you say, "Yes" to inappropriate requests, you are saying, "No" to God's Spirit and "No" to your health and well-being.

A complicated life makes depression worse. You may benefit from choosing to disconnect from some *optional* aspects of life. Parenting, employment, church attendance, and prayer are not optional aspects of life.

---

[41] Hennigan, Bruce; Sutton, Mark, *Conquering Depression – A 30-Day Plan to Find Happiness* (Nashville, TN; B & H Publishing, 2001) p. 112

## A Bit Personal

Some years back all was not well. My symptoms of depression were constant. To put this in perspective, I had no reason to be depressed. Our sons, Lane, Chris were healthy as was my wife Norma. Truth Tabernacle (later re-doctrined and re-branded Courageous, 2848 North Broadway; Springfield, MO.) was growing. Plans were in place to build an auditorium, a building the group still benefits from. Some of my early books were actually selling. Invitations were coming to speak at various events. Life was good.

But it wasn't. Few people knew my struggle. Each Sunday, I pulled everything together to be "normal." While I struggled people were being born again. The church was progressing.

On Monday, regardless of Sunday's impact I was *under-water*. It was not the, "more pastors resign on Monday than on Sunday" stuff. On Monday, I would be dysfunctional. Normal life was exhausting. Sunday had spent my "normal." I lived day to day. By Wednesday I'd be able to pull enough together to again tackle public life.

What I describe is a hard way to live. It was not just hard for me. It was hard for Norma. I'm sure it was hard on Lane and Chris. How could it not be? Their dad who was perceived as iconic by a handful of mistaken people was a shadow at home. At home, their dad would be barely responsive, not having enough energy to play basketball. A dark bedroom was my comfort zone.

In time, I had gone as far as I could. A counselor helped, but I also benefitted from simplifying my life.

## Simple is Good!

At the time, I participated in a missions program requiring me to travel overseas each year. There were other involvements on community boards and with my church organization. Individually, none were overwhelming. Collectively, they added weight to my struggle.

Simplifying meant leaving behind non-essentials. It meant:

1. Resigning every non-essential role that required me to expend energy.

2. Establishing routines that became habit. Habits help because they require little thought.
3. Each day was regimented. Awaken, take one or both of our sons to school. Return home to dress for the day. On to a breakfast café, for coffee, morning newspaper, a slow breakfast and reviewing the tasks for the day. Then to the office, for prayer time - using a prayer journaling approach.
4. The rest of the day was more flexible. But, I started each day with simple repetitive actions that became habitual.

"Simplify" also meant I did not attend every event at the church I pastored. Many district and sectional events happened without me being present. Simplifying life helped me battle depression.

For you to accomplish this simplification process, start by looking at your life from 360 degrees. What unnecessary (or less important) things are consuming your time and energy? Perhaps some social media accounts need to be eliminated. Are certain forums that have evolved into debate good for your mind and emotions? Could some projects that have you over-extended wait a bit? You may need to write a few letters of resignation. Get rid of all unnecessary baggage.

Beyond stepping away from some activity, establishing routines will help.

## Simplify – Cave Living

Perhaps it was doing the essentials that helped Elijah survive his depression, (1 Kings 19:5-8). While sitting alone in the wilderness, Elijah prayed to die. His appeal went unanswered. (It is also interesting and informative of God's patience, that Elijah's prayer to die received no rebuke from the Lord.)

While Elijah was in that condition, it seems God temporarily relieved Elijah of his prophetic responsibility. For an extended time, Elijah made no ringing pronouncements. He did not challenge any prophets of false gods, did not rebuke Ahab or Jezebel, and Elijah is not seen praying for drought or rain. Elijah was living a simple life.

In time, Elijah relocated to a cave. He was still alone. Still despairing of life. Had Elijah backslidden? No! Elijah had not backslidden. Elijah was simply being human.

Events in Elijah's life had positioned him for a downturn. The prophet had expended much emotion, energy, and adrenaline in the contest with the prophets of Baal. Elijah needed a season of simple! Elijah's prayer was not answered. He did not die. In time, he was again accomplishing meaningful things for God. But in the season of the cave, Elijah needed simple.

## You May Need Simple!

Such seasons of simplifying call for:

1. Getting rid of extras.
2. Taking time for yourself, including getting good sleep.
3. Eating a reasonably healthy diet.
4. Doing the things that renew your vitality. These are the things that renew your spirit.

## Simplify – Reduce the Flood of Information

We get too much data. In 1970, news arrived at my parent's home one time per day. It came via the *Alexandria Daily Town Talk* tossed on our drive. I'd read almost every word of the *Town Talk*. Vietnam was in full swing, desegregation had just come to Central Louisiana, there were anti-war riots in major cities, and "rock and roll" were in the entertainment headlines.

My favorite part of the *Town Talk* was the sports section, but I read it all, including Ann Landers' daily column. In those days, even for those who owned a television, information was slow to arrive.

Today, there is an unceasing torrent of information. Media sources provide an ongoing flood of updates: CNN, Fox News, Alt-right, Alt-left, Huffington Post, gossip forums, and Social media posts. Much is trivial at best and silly at worst.

For 24 hours of each day, 365 days of each year, you can choose to be listening to a conversation about politics, sports, finances, government, entertainment, weight-loss or a myriad of other topics. A flow of such insignificant information agitates the mind, emotion and spirit. It is not the prescription for a simple life!

Being in control, means you can make a choice to not listen, read or watch.

- Do you need every messenger app? To simplify you probably need to delete several paths of communication.
- Why do you still get email you signed up for, but never open? Simplify by having your email address removed.
- The commute to work by car, subway, bus, plane, ferry or Uber could be used to listen to your flavor of "talk show." Most of what you hear won't be good. The opinions on politics, sports and business are just that – opinions. Do they really matter? To simplify would be to take the time to think or meditate on the Bible.

Escaping the deluge of information will require intentional withdrawal. Turn off text alerts. Don't have your email and social media accounts on every device. To simplify will almost certainly mean to "unplug" from quite a bit of life.

### Simplify – Establish Sabbath

Sabbath is part of the Ten Commandments. Sabbath was and is simplicity. After God completed His creation work, He rested. If God rested, how much do we need rest?

Rest for each person is different. Sabbath involves doing some things you enjoy that reduces stress. Your Sabbath may be fulfilled by "doing nothing." If so, without guilt – do nothing.

- Nap, read, and nap some more.
- Take a pajama day.
- Read a book in a long hot bath.
- Go bird-watching.
- Take a walk in the woods.
- Go "flea-marketing" or visit yard sales.
- Take a day trip to an Amish community.
- Chop wood, at least if chopping wood does not feel like work to you.
- Spend time with flowers or gardening if that is enjoyable.

In ancient Israel, Sabbath was simple. It happened each week. At our home, there seems to be no way to make one day untouchable as a "day off." Instead, we have to take our Sabbath breaks in "week-long" bites. Those weeks don't happen often enough. They only happen if we put them on our calendar. When we take those several days, it helps dampen the smoldering flame that becomes a consuming fire of "too much." "Too much" leads to exhaustion, which is a fertile field in which depression often takes root.

### Simplify – Constrain Yourself

To simplify, you may have to give your spouse or a friend, your phone, tablet, and laptop computer for a defined period of time. Another option is *Cold Turkey,* an app and program designed to limit time wasters on electronic devices.

In the battle with depression - any win works as a start. Even the win of stopping some of the things you now do.

# Chapter 16
# Mapping an Unwanted Journey

In seasons of depression, well-meaning people offer advice like, "Pray your way through it," or the more frustrating, "What is wrong with you? You have a wonderful life – you need to give God praise!"

Decades ago, I might have given similar suggestions. A novice preacher recently graced our pulpit. He offered such advice. Like the younger version of me, he was providing a travel review to a destination he had never visited.

Having now repeatedly traveled to the dark place, I'm a much better travel guide for someone else's journey into and out of depression.

### You Never Travel Alone

A descriptive word the Lord Jesus Christ used for the Holy Spirit is the Greek word *paraclete*. The word, often translated "comforter" by the KJV, described someone who comes alongside to help another.

The Spirit of Christ is no fair-weather friend. As you battle depression, Jesus' Spirit is there. You may not feel His presence, but know Him to be alongside. To trust when you cannot feel is faith at work.

Engrave one verse of God's Word on your mind. Make it a giant poster for your emotions. It is the words:

*...I will never leave thee nor forsake thee.*
**Hebrews 13:5**

I have found myself muttering, "I'm not alone in this!" In dark moments, I've done some inner shouting, "Where are you, God? It's dark down here." Those are my words, but when faith speaks – it speaks words of assurance and consolation.

Being mindful of Christ's Spirit does not necessarily make depression easier. It does offer support in the struggle.

## Dark Places Create Brilliance

Since creation, light has not existed alone. Darkness completes the cycle. Darkness is necessary.

Dark seasons are a significant part of the making of life. A potter's clay creation, so masterfully spun, does not take on rich shades of silver, red, or yellow, until a time of being fired in a dark furnace occurs.

A hot, gloomy kiln births brilliant color. David, Elijah, Job, Charles Spurgeon, Abraham Lincoln, and other exceptional people battled the darkness. To what degree is the dark kiln of depression the making of a man?

The dark place has been the birthplace of some of my best sermons, creative ideas, Bible Studies, and writing. At times when I have preached on encouragement, faith or victory through Christ, I preached primarily to myself. Later, notes came from distant places telling how much that particular sermon had helped someone else.

Battling the dark despair of depression adds color to a life that might otherwise be faded and dingy. It is not depression that produces the color, it is the battle against depression.

Knowing the positive results that can come from the battle against depression does not make the struggle enjoyable. Instead, that knowledge does give some purpose to the pain.

## Thinking About and Seeking After God

The 143rd Psalm is one of David's seven penitential psalms. David's frustration with life used words and phrases with which depressed people will be familiar:

> *... the enemy hath ... smitten my life down to the ground;*
> *he hath made me to dwell in darkness, ...*
> *Therefore is my spirit overwhelmed within me ...*
> **Psalms 143:3-4**

The words were David's honest feelings. As we deal with depression we must be equally honest. Notice: David does not stop with what he can feel; he moves on to things remembered,

84

*I remember the days of old; I meditate (the word translated "meditate"*
*means to murmur or to talk to oneself) on all thy works;*
*I muse on the work of thy hands. I stretch forth my hands unto thee:*
*my soul thirsteth after thee, as a thirsty land…*
**Psalms 143:5-6**

In his dark place, David saturated his thoughts with remembering and "talking to himself" about God's works. David also focused his desire on one thing. He reached out for God as a longing child reaches for a parent. He thirsted after God like a dry land seeks water.

David's depression pressed Him to seek for His God. Our depression must move us to do the same. The search cannot be based on seeking a particular feeling or emotion. Instead we will simply seek after Him and reflect on His works.

## Going the Right Direction

It is easy to get lost when traveling to new destinations. No landmark is familiar. A flight connection took me through Hong Kong. It required an overnight stay. When my plane landed, I discovered my hotel was on the mainland. No taxi at the airport traveled to where my hotel was located. My only option was to take a bus.

The hotel was an unknown destination, the bus would travel an unknown route, there was no assurance that any fellow-traveler spoke my language, my ability in the Mandarin language is non-existent, so every sign was in an unknown language. It was late.

I'm usually ready to tackle almost anything. I'm seldom afraid and at times friends and family think I'm incautious. In Hong Kong, wisdom prevailed. On this occasion, I had no idea if I'd be traveling in the right direction and making the right bus connections. My prepaid hotel reservation ended up as money lost. I slept on a bench in the Hong Kong airport.

Why? I had no sense of direction or point of reference.

Left unfought, depression similarly leaves you with no sense of direction or point of reference. Depression disables the GPS of the human spirit. There is no feeling for where you are, or even if you are going in the right direction. Your emotional trauma; satan, the accuser of the brethren; shame and insecurity will all attempt to convince that you are off course.

Don't listen. A dark season of depression does not mean you are carnal, backslidden, or unspiritual. Since you know prayer is the right thing to do – pray on! Because you know daily devotion is proper – maintain your devotion. Since attending worship services and Bible teaching is beneficial – attend! At the moment, your emotions may tell you that none of these things have value, but they do.

Let the psalmist affirm these truths:

*If I ascend up into heaven, thou art there: if I make my bed in hell, behold, thou art there. If I take the wings of the morning, and dwell in the uttermost parts of the sea;... If I say, Surely the darkness shall cover me; even the night shall be light about me. Yea, the darkness hideth not from thee; but the night shineth as the day: the darkness and the light are both alike to thee.*
**Psalm 139:8-12**

Come on. Endure, survive, and then thrive. God does not see you as a failure. To God, who divided dark from light, the darkness and light are both essential to His creation. Endure the darkness – in time the dawn will come.

# Chapter 17
# Look Behind the Green Screen

Depression is to the mind and emotions like the physical experience of walking through a swamp. As a teen, on occasion, I would go duck-hunting in a Louisiana swamp. At times, I would walk several hundred yards through water mid-thigh, with mud sucking at every step.

Wading through a swamp is muddy, messy, slow, and exhausting. Depression is also muddy, messy, slow, and exhausting.

## The Swamp Extends Forever

At the end of the day, as a duck-hunter trudges back to the high ground, he can see and know the dry ground is ahead. The swamp of depression differs in that it seems perpetual.

In depression, the swamp extends in every direction as far as you can see. It is a mental and emotional trip through hip-deep water with muck sucking at your boots each step.

In such times, it seems as if life does not exist beyond depression. When the swamp is the only thing you can see, it generates exhaustion and despair. The swamp of depression is real. It is exhausting and debilitating.

But those battling depression need an expanded perception.

## Depression Creates a "Green Screen"

The use of a "green screen" is a technique of photographing or filming a person or object in front of a green monochrome backdrop. With the use of technology, a different image then replaces the monochrome backdrop.

The cowboy in an ad for Levi's jeans may be shown to be in the desert. The fellow may not have been within 500 miles of a desert when the picture was taken, Photographic sleight-of-hand created the look for the advertisement.

Perceiving your depression as a perpetual swamp is an unreal snapshot of life. Having lived it, I am not suggesting depression is fake. These defining characteristics of depression attest to its reality for someone experiencing it:

- Sadness without reason
- Lack of motivation
- A sense of helplessness
- Worthlessness
- Hopelessness
- Lack of focus
- Less energy than usual
- No pleasure in things you have previously enjoyed.
- The struggle to maintain normal social activities.

All are real. These characteristics have you feeling like you are walking through a never-ending swamp. And those feelings are not fake. They are as real as this morning's sunrise.

**Depression's Green Screen**

But like the green screen, depression does not tell the true story. In depression, when you look ahead – you see the swamp. It extends as far as you can see. Look behind you, and it seems you have been in this swamp forever.

It seems all of life has been spent in this dreadful place named depression. You may have done grand things, but anything you have accomplished has no value while you are in the swamp of depression. You feel your life to have been a total failure.

Depression's "green screen" also seems to indicate that your struggle will be there for every tomorrow. The idea that depression will last forever is debilitating. A person who has battled depression in the past and is having another season struggles with the thought, "What if I don't come out of it this time?"

Depression's false tale is that you have been depressed forever and that your life has never had value. It is a lie. It is depression's "green screen."

**Past Success is Today's Encouragement**

All past survival is a source of present encouragement. Many will have already endured depression. In your previous journey through depression, didn't it seem as though the marsh would never end? You felt hopeless then as well.

Yet, you came out of it. Most people do. Your earlier depression may have lasted six months, a year, or five years. It wasn't easy, but you survived. Remembering yesterday's survival will help you make it now.

## Think about Life

For a moment, minimize your feeling and maximize your thinking. What we "think" and what we "feel" are not the same thing. Emotions can be illogical.

Look at your calendar. Before you walked into this swamp of depression, what coming event would have brought you joy? Will a grandchild soon be born? Is college graduation just ahead? Perhaps, a conference you have always enjoyed awaits. Possibly, some of your "best friends" are coming to town.

You are thinking, "Sir, the idea of spending time with anybody or going to any event is exhausting." Remember, in this exercise you are not feeling. You are "thinking."

There is value and joy in all the things you know you to be worthy of celebration. Even if you do not feel like celebrating them just now. Somewhere ahead are better times. There is a reason to slog on through your swamp.

## Think about the Past

Again, limit your feelings and think. Open the pictures and videos on your phone or get a box of old photos from a closet. Look at the pictures. Think about what you are seeing. Close your eyes and relive the smells and sounds. Let the moving pictures of memory play on the big screen in your mind.

Some examples from my world:

- Pictures of Lane and Chris as boys.
- A picture of our two grandsons. Kaden and Wyatt at three years old as they are having a whispered conversation on the drive leading to our home. About what were three-year-olds whispering?

- The pictures of mine and Norma's wedding.
- A framed copy of my first published book, *Daily Things of Christian Living*.[42]
- A picture of Norma's record album from those days when we evangelized.
- A video clip of Elsie, our grand-daughter, when at 18-months old she discovers her shadow on a wall. Her response was to head-butt her shadow.

Looking at the pictures and videos gives me a peek around the green screen. My life has been richly satisfying. Pictures of experiences shared with "laughing friends" like Stan and Melba, Tim and Joan, Jerry and Phyllis, Perry and Loretta, or Roy and Debbie, help put life in perspective.

It reminds me. I have not always been in the swamp. In the past, I have laughed till my sides hurt. I will laugh again.

Try it. As you look at your pictures and videos – remember.

---

[42] *Daily Things of Christian Living* is out of print. An updated version will be released.

# Chapter 18
# Was a Blacksmith Ever Depressed?

Earlier generations may not have had the amount of depression common today. Depression certainly existed. As already mentioned, in earlier times presidents, musicians, prophets, and preachers of renown dealt with depression.

At the same time, we can surmise that a large percentage of the population did not deal with depression. It is also possible, that depression existed widely, but was not discussed.

What is certain is the correlation between physical exertion and depression. Until the 1950s, in North America most labor was manual. Outside the western hemisphere this is often still the case. A logger, farmer, home-maker, or blacksmith worked hard. Air-conditioning did not exist. Sweat was the currency of accomplishment. Even the most genteel job happened in buildings hot in summer and frigid in winter. People were often physically tired at day's end. Home-makers who toiled at a wood stove, washed clothes by hand and daily pulled weeds from the garden were physically exhausted.

Our world has more "thought work." Tractors and factories are air-conditioned. The washing machine has replaced the scrub-board. Some people work before a computer screen for many hours each week.

Such work *is* taxing, but it is not a "good exhaustion." Those who do sedentary work end the workday with pent-up energy stored in the large muscle groups of the body. We are, "mentally tired, but physically restless."[43]

In earlier days, the people spoken of as being depressed were poets, artists, authors, teachers, and political leaders. I have not yet read of a depressed blacksmith, carpenter, or store-keeper. Hard physical activity seemed to help prevent the depths of depression.

---

[43] Hazard p. 83.

## A Moving Body and a Healthy Mind

A University of California at Berkeley, School of Public Health's ongoing survey shows a strong association between a sedentary lifestyle and depression.

If your output of physical energy is low, you are two times as likely to slump into depression as a person getting even modest exercise. Someone who exercises more intensely (intense bicycling, weight-lifting, aerobics, swimming) is even less likely to experience depression.[44]

Studies like those at the University of California at Berkeley have shown that exercise is necessary, in fact almost mandatory, in the battle against depression. Structured exercise even challenges the slow movements common in those who are depressed.

Psychologists at Duke University, did research involving 156 older adults with mild to moderate depression. The researchers randomly assigned people to one of three groups.

- One group exercised three times each week for 45 minutes.
- A second group exercised and took an antidepressant.
- The third group took only the medicine.

After four months, researchers found that the people who exercised, but took no medicine, showed the same improvement as those who did either of the other treatment plans.

Continued tracking showed that those who continued exercising were less likely to experience recurrent depression than were either of the other two groups.[45]

It is clear that exercise helps eliminate toxins from both the body and mind.

## Why Exercise Helps with Depression

Biochemicals are not limited to any particular area of the human body. As a person gets involved in a physical effort – whether as a blacksmith or lifting weights – endorphins are released.

---

[44] Hazard, p. 84
[45] Mayo p. 113

These endorphins come from the nerves working with the exercising muscle. The goal of these endorphins is to limit the pain associated with the exertion. When this happens, there are not only enough endorphins released to respond to the pain; it is as though there is a flood of endorphins. These extra endorphins become available to serve as the bridges between nerve endings in the brain.

Studies also show that the exercise of muscles increases the levels of serotonin in the brain. Further, exercise you do today can have an effect that lasts for two weeks. It is proven that a <u>consistent</u> fitness plan can be as effective in dealing with moderate depression as is an anti-depressant medication.

## Honor God With Your Body

*Warning! Warning!* The words ahead have potential to add to your current depression. Since these are God's words, they may also quicken you to action.

Paul instructed the Corinthians to honor God in their body.

> *What? know ye not that your body is the temple of the Holy Ghost*
> *which is in you, which ye have of God, and ye are not your own?*
> *For ye are bought with a price: therefore glorify God in your body,*
> *and in your spirit, which are God's.*
> **1 Corinthians 6:19-20**

When you are not overwhelmingly depressed, take a look in the mirror. Is God honored by "that body?" The look in the mirror is not about feeling shame or disgust. It is a catalyst for action. When a 45-year-old person looks in the mirror, the reflection does not show the muscle tone of a 26-year-old. Life, time, and gravity make an impact. Shame is not the objective. Don't compare yourself to anyone else.

But, if we are not glorifying God in our body and spirit, could we not use Paul's words as an impetus for improvement? Regarding overcoming depression, entering some exercise effort helps. It will also benefit, in that your body may well begin to glorify God.

## Do Something Physical

Few who read this will decide to start a new career as a blacksmith. Since such a career is not likely, the other option is to engage in a consistent fitness program.

Exercise helps deal with stress. The body gets a lift from regular sweat-inducing exercise. I'm competitive by nature. My best approach is anything competitive. Basketball with people near my age, tennis, racquetball or *walking* 18 holes of golf benefit me. When at our best, my wife and I frequent a county-owned fitness center. It has every fitness machine imaginable.

There is simply no excuse to not do something physical. Walking and biking trails abound. Health permitting, do something to raise your heart rate. Physical exertion also increases your energy level and lifts your mood.

Taking advantage of the connection between physical effort and mental well-being requires effort. The work for the benefit of your body and emotions does not just happen. You must:

- Get started. Even fifteen minutes on a treadmill or shooting a basketball is a start.
- Do it again tomorrow. Repetition is the foundation of habits.
- Make your fitness a principal goal. The goal is not to be Mr. Atlas or Ms. World. The goal IS to be fit – glorifying God in your body.
- Create a sustainable physical workout plan that fits you and your life.
- Adjust your workout. Otherwise, it becomes boring and non-sustainable.

In essence – do something. Get moving, whether you feel like it or not. Paul wrote,

*For bodily exercise profiteth little…*
**1 Timothy 4:8**

Paul did not say, "bodily exercise is of no profit." If for nothing more than mental health, exercise has benefit.

## Have a Partner in Your Effort

It is hard for a depressed person to launch something like what is suggested. To get more leverage for getting started, recruit a partner with whom to walk, jog, ride bikes, golf, chop wood, or work-out.

Having a partner makes anything easier. For some years, I played racquetball with a friend who leads a major Christian organization. We are both competitive, both live stress-filled lives, and both need exercise (as well as on occasion needing the opportunity to hit something – really hard). The partnership in exercise worked. Our participation together added a measure of accountability.

Keeping active, being fit, and eating a balanced diet may not be the complete solution to dealing with depression. However, these three things often contribute to a sense of mental well-being.

# Chapter 19
# Get Outside

We can all benefit from God's creation. No human engineering or ingenuity can match the brilliance of what happened when,

*And God said . . .*
**Genesis 1:3**

Depression thrives in darkness or surrounded by plastic and aluminum. Depression seems more comfortable at a distance from God's creation.

Elijah moved his despair and feelings of failure to a cave. Earlier, he had been alongside a brook. By the brook, he had been outside, where the birds flew and the wind blew. Perhaps, this season of Elijah's life would have lasted fewer than forty days if he had remained outside a bit longer.

Being outside helps deal with my depression. It may be the quietness of reading while sitting in a swing beneath our arbor. Mowing or being on our old 16.5 horsepower Kubota tractor is all therapy for my mind.

My Grandfather went through a difficult season, lasting for several years. "Granny" had been injured in an auto crash and then diagnosed with Parkinson's disease. Her illness slowly progressed. Part of Grandpa's remedy for coping was walking a trail cut in the pasture behind their home. Several times each day he walked that path. As he walked, he meditated on life and prayed. Being outside was part of his response to the challenge presented to him.

Travis Miller, a former co-worker now pastoring in Seattle, re-introduced me to the pleasure of biking. It helps. Being on a bike slows the pace of my life. Things I had never noticed became an enjoyment to watch. It is almost a return to childhood. There were places to go, neighborhoods to explore, and trails to ride. Something special happens when the sun is beating down and the wind is blowing in your face. If you don't care for walking, or like me, cannot imagine jogging as being enjoyable, give bicycling a try.

Planting a garden is also therapeutic. Having dirt under my fingernails became an unexpected pleasure. Doing battle with raccoons and deer, both of whom seem to know exactly when the corn ripens forces me to think outside the office.

For married couples, it is ideal if both can be outside together. Many cities and towns have scenic walking paths. Take advantage of them. As you walk, watch the birds or butterflies. Norma and I have a book in which we've marked the birds we've seen. Notice the flowers. Be outside to participate in the changing of leaves each fall. Doing something to get yourself outside has potential to help you battle depression.

## Work Outside

When circumstances have me set for an episode of depression, I intentionally plan to work outside. It is also intentional that it be hard physical work.

As is the case with exercise, hard work boils the toxins from my system. Clearing a fence-row, or sealing an asphalt drive reduces depression's impact. The depression still comes, but low emotions and mental condition do not own the moment. I've picked a path to get ahead of the darkness.

My skills are limited. I'm not a builder or craftsman. But, I can pull weeds from the water garden. I'm also able to clean up and reorganize the barn.

Tired muscles help a struggling mind.

## Small Bites Please

Let me add an insight. While battling depression, don't tackle a three-week project. If your therapy is sealing a drive, purchase as much asphalt sealer as can be applied in one day. This may seem counter-intuitive. We think, "There is far more here than can be accomplished in a day. I'll focus over the next few days and get it all done."

Remember though, even as you use physical labor to battle your depression, the depression remains. It may be that after you make the big plan, debilitating depression wins for a day, two days or even three. Some days, there is scarcely enough energy to put on your shoes. On those days, you will not apply asphalt sealer or rearrange the cupboard.

When you have no energy, your unfinished project becomes another failure. It may be weeks or months before you have the time, energy, and inclination to again tackle the project. Small bites please!

# Chapter 20
# "Be Prepared"

Scouting programs use the motto:  **Be Prepared**. In scouting, the phrase means two things

- **Be Prepared in Mind** by having disciplined yourself to be obedient to every order, and also by having thought out beforehand any accident or situation that might occur, so that you know the right thing to do at the right moment, and are willing to do it.
- **Be Prepared in Body** by making yourself strong and active and able to do the right thing at the right moment.[46]

"Be prepared" applies to much of life. This includes depression. This is particularly true for anyone having a history of depression.

In 1995, a June edition of *Time* magazine had a picture of Scott O'Grady on the front. On June 2, the plane Scott O'Grady was flying was shot down over Bosnia. He parachuted into enemy territory. Upon landing, O'Grady was frightened. Any of us would have been.

Then Scott O'Grady remembered his training. He had been equipped and prepared for this exact experience. His sense of confidence began to return. Being behind enemy lines in Bosnia was not a desirable situation, but O'Grady knew he was prepared. Scott O'Grady began to act as he had been trained. It worked. The enemy did not capture him.

Six days later, rescuers arrived. Captain O'Grady returned home a hero. Scott O'Grady survived because of having prepared for a problem that eventually arose.

## Wisdom Says Prepare

The Bible is big on the concept of preparation. Ants and builders exemplify those who properly prepare.

---

[46] Baden-Powell, Robert, *Scouting for Boys – Campfire Yarn No. 3 – Becoming a Scout.*

It is seen in Solomon's wisdom:

*Go to the ant, thou sluggard; consider her ways, and be wise:*
*Which having no guide, overseer, or ruler, Provideth her meat*
*in the summer, and gathereth her food in the harvest.*
**Proverbs 6:6-8**

Jesus saw preparation as being important:

*For which of you, intending to build a tower, sitteth not down first, and*
*counteth the cost, whether he have sufficient to finish it? Lest haply, after he*
*hath laid the foundation, and is not able to finish it, all that behold it begin*
*to mock him, Saying, This man began to build, and was not able to finish.*
**Luke 14:28-30**

We can prepare for much that life brings.

- Firemen encourage families to train their children for a possible fire.
- Tornado preparedness is a regular conversation in the Midwestern United States.
- Millions of books are sold to prepare students to take college entrance exams.
- Heart patients are prepared. They have nitroglycerin tablets nearby.

Such preparation is not faithless. Preparation is wise whether dealing with a tornado or depression.

Those who have fought depression have a significant danger of another encounter. Like Scott O'Grady or someone with a heart condition, be prepared.

## How to Be Prepared

Some suggestions for preparing for depression come from Martin Luther. Luther wrote of symptoms now identified with depression. Luther's biographers say he battled low self-esteem which, like fatigue, is fertile soil for depression.

Luther's ideas for being prepared to overcome depression included:

1. Avoid being alone.
2. Seek help from others.
3. Sing or make music.
4. Praise and give thanks.
5. Lean heavily on the power of God's Word.
6. Rest confidently in the presence of God's Spirit.

Notice that Luther's suggestions are a mix of the practical and the spiritual. These are all things a person can prepare to do before depression hits. And as Luther's list suggests, depression should be addressed from all angles – the physical, emotional, mental and spiritual.

**Know the Settings for Depression**

Some veterans of depression could wear many battle ribbons. If you are one of those, try learning the sort of circumstances that bring you to depression.

Holiday Depression

The time around Christmas and New Year depresses many people. These holidays are portrayed idealistically. Christmas' reality seldom matches the ideal.

Families gather. For some, such gatherings reopen old wounds. Other families enjoy each other's company, but are made sad at separating. This is particularly true when a family member is terminally ill, or as elders slow a bit.

People then depart the holidays feeling depressed. An anticipated high point of life has failed them again.

Knowing a holiday season might leave you depressed should be encouragement to prepare yourself for those days and the aftermath of those days.

After Major Accomplishments

After completing a major project, weariness and adrenal fatigue can become depression. For an author, it may be the completion of a book. A couple building their dream home can move in and one or the other soon struggle with depression.

Some people enjoy the *next* challenge. If so, some help may come from thinking about your next objective. Of course, it is not best to immediately tackle another major project. But, thinking about tomorrow's goals can help in the war with depression.

## Exhaustion

A business executive working seventy hours per week, anyone working two jobs, or parents with a newborn experience weariness. Fatigue affects body, mind, spirit, and emotions. Consistently getting only five hours of sleep throws the door open and puts out a welcome mat for depression.

Where possible, balance work, play, and relaxation. There are times when balance is not possible. But for someone who struggles with depression to repeatedly over-commit to work while getting little sleep is folly. The mother of a newborn has little choice in her schedule. Most other people do.

The best solution: schedule time off on your calendar. Force yourself to take Sabbath time. Those who have a driven personality will not take breaks from work, if those breaks are not scheduled.

## Other Seasons

There are other potential seasons of depression. A person can anticipate and prepare for most:

- The aftermath of a major surgery.
- Disappointment with a job situation.
- A family relationship that has gone bad.

If you repeatedly deal with depression, be watchful for early warning signs!

Often, I know if the darkness of depression is drawing near. My early signs include:

- Lacking energy when there is no reason to be exhausted.

- Seeking to be alone more than usual. As an introvert, my batteries recharge while I'm alone. An early indicator of impending depression is to more acutely desire to be alone.

Your early warnings will be different. You need to learn what those indicators are. As depression looms, take the actions you have already planned. Be prepared!

Use the space below to write down traits you deem to be "early warnings." Do your best to never be surprised by the onset of depression.

_____

_____

_____

_____

_____

_____

_____

_____

**Prepare Your Response**

Scott O'Grady survived a difficult experience. As a military pilot, O'Grady was aware of the possibility of such a crash. More importantly, he was prepared to respond.

O'Grady's preparation for a crash behind enemy lines began long before he needed it. How wise similar preparation is for anyone prone to depression. Plan your strategy and actions for dealing with depression.

- What are the situations or seasons that move you toward depression?
- What are the early signs of impending depression?
- What will you do if and when those warning signs begin to occur?
- What is your planned response? How will you fight back?

My approach may not work for you. My strategy includes:

1. Giving myself a good talking to. It is a bit like a pep talk before an athletic team takes the field. "Carlton, it is about to happen again. You are going to go through it. You will not lie down and let depression run over you. Get ready to fight every day. Fight, regardless of how you feel. There may be days when you don't win the battle, but you won't quit."
2. Hard physical work. In my work-life, I have done mostly "white collar" work. When depression lurks, it is a good time to trim trees or clear a fence row. If string is needed for the weed-eater, it is bought ahead of the full storm of depression. When depression is full-on, I may not have enough energy to visit a home improvement center. It is also not likely that I will go, because I don't want to interact with people.
3. As depression gets close, I have close friends or family members who know my struggle. I'll alert several by text message that the battle is on. These men pray and provide a level of compassionate care.
4. Certain people help with the battle. Our grandkids almost always help without them knowing it. A child's enthusiasm for life is a bit contagious.

## Gather Your Resources Ahead of Time

You can't build a storm shelter while a tornado bears down. When an episode of Major Depressive Disorder hits, it is too late to prepare. Being prepared won't necessarily lighten depression or eliminate any symptom. Following the motto, "Be prepared," does give you a process for recovery.

When I'm depressed the work moves slowly. Sealing the drive will take twice as long as it would if I were not depressed. Though moving frustratingly slow, I'm still moving. As said repeatedly, while fighting depression any activity is a win.

## Your Plan

God created each of us to be unique. My specific plan won't work for you, but the strategy, "Be prepared," probably will.

Knowing yourself, what resources do you need? Will a certain sort of music help? Does reading self-help material like that written by Norman Vincent Peale help? Is there a confidante to whom you should talk? Will it help to detox your body, eliminating sugar from your diet? Might a mental detox – fasting social media and video games be part of your strategy?

The message here is: "You must be prepared in some way if you want to win the battle with depression."

## Think it Through

Imagine you are Scott O'Grady, except your challenge is not preparing for a crash-landing in Bosnia. You are preparing for specific actions you will take to survive and overcome depression. What will you do?

# Chapter 21
# Don't Make Unnecessary Decisions

While depressed, do not make major life-changing decisions.

Life looks bleaker during depression. A false shade of gray filters life. Things look worse than they are.

Everything seems to be a mess. In reality, the only thing messed up may be your own emotions and state of mind. Thus, any decision is being made based on false accounting.

**Don't do it!**

Depressed people should not:

- Quit their job.
- Resign a pastorate.
- Leave their spouse.
- Buy a new car or boat.
- Change colleges or change their college major.
- Start a new business venture.
- Pull a "geographic," believing things will be better "somewhere else."
- Change churches.
- Abandon Godly lifestyle choices in hopes of easing their pain.

While depressed: defer, defer, defer. Put off decisions as long as possible. Some people will think you to be indecisive. Don't let anyone coerce you into making a decision while depressed. It is better to be temporarily indecisive than to be permanently stuck with a bad decision.

At times, life comes in ways where decisions cannot be deferred. When this happens, get counsel from a wise person who has nothing to gain or lose from the decision you must make. This "wise" person needs to have been relatively effective in their life, career, and relationships. Don't seek marriage advice from someone who has been divorced three times. Don't seek career advice from someone incapable of keeping a job. Don't seek spiritual direction from someone who has no prayer life and never reads the Bible.

# Chapter 22
# Vitamins for Mind & Emotions

In her later years, Nona Freeman, an incredible missionary to Africa, became known for the vitamins she took. At times, the dear lady had a large bag of vitamins in her even larger purse. I've sat at lunch watching with amazement as she sorted out her vitamins and those for her husband.

Her "vitamizing" must have worked. The Freemans both lived long, active lives. In time, Nona Freeman wrote a booklet about the benefits of various vitamins.

Taking vitamins is a response to a deficiency in the human body. Due to improper diet or the body not processing food correctly, the human body is not receiving enough of a needed substance.

## Mental Vitamins

In a similar way, depressed people can benefit from "mental vitamins." Mental vitamins are anything that can speak a positive word into your life and mind.

## Vitamin #1 - Educate Yourself

My mother has battled Rheumatoid Arthritis (RA) for decades. Mom has read everything available about RA. She does not depend on a doctor knowing the latest. Mom has thus improved her options and health.

It has been said of those who deal with depression, "We have to know what we are fighting to win the war."[47] Read books, magazine articles, or listen to podcasts about depression. Depression must be understood to be overcome.[48] This strategy is an important vitamin. Insight is often the cure for a troubled mind.[49]

(A caveat is needed: as you read or listen, don't seize on every crackpot theory that comes along.)

---

[47] Keen p.51
[48] Maughon p. 36
[49] Ibid, p. 31.

When in the swamp of depression, there is little energy to educate yourself about depression. But do your best. Even if you read half of a page each day, go ahead and read. Learning more about depression will position you to survive.

When you have more energy, read extensively about what you just experienced. Hopefully, you never again experience depression. If you don't, it is likely that someone you know will. Your experience with depression and knowledge on the subject will be of benefit to someone.

## Vitamin #2 – Anything Positive

Motivational books are mental vitamins for some people. For others, such books are an irritant. For me, studying the Bible with depth is a mental vitamin. It is one of those, "what's good for Carlton" things.

Time spent with positive people who make no judgments are part of "anything positive." During one quite severe bouts of depression, Norma and I were with life-long friends. As he and I would talk, there were times when what I was trying to say would not come together. An idea was there. The right words to express my idea would not come. It was frustrating. He knew it was. His positive response was simply, "That's ok, Carlton, it'll come."

## Vitamin #3 - Travel

Travel opportunities can be a vitamin for the mind. Not every person has this sort of opportunity. But travel does not require an airplane or visiting another continent. A daytrip of thirty miles may be of help.

A pastor friend has been dealt several unfair blows. Preaching in his home pulpit does not relieve his long-standing depression. However, preaching in some other pulpit, even a few dozen miles away energizes him. Traveling and preaching in those settings is a vitamin for his mind.

These are suggestions to help you think about your own "vitamins." The vitamin for your mind may be bird-watching or horse-back riding. Whatever puts some positives in your spirit - do it.

# Chapter 23
## Pray – Differently

An evangelist friend encouraged me to complete this book. He had listened to a Christian talk show. Someone called in about their struggle with depression. The host and guests derided the caller and suggested what they needed was more prayer. Their unkind responses made my friend angry.

It is a fool who denigrates prayer. The identity of the church I'm part of is that of being a praying church. Prayer is needed. Prayer is essential. Prayer is a non-negotiable whether in a valley or on a mountain.

Depression may be spiritual. But not always. Prayer in and of itself will not necessarily fix depression. An extended fast will not necessarily cure depression. There are certainly other benefits added to a person's life as a result of both prayer and fasting. So, pray on and fast on!

### A Mature Understanding of Prayer

"Feelings" are not the basis for effective prayer; just as feeling are not always the outcome of effective prayer. A prayer-life driven by emotion disappears when a person is "down." Prayer is not to be dependent on how you feel or whether you feel the nearness of God.

A depressed person must not stop praying. In His *Sermon on the Mount*, Jesus said, "*When* ye pray . . .." He said this three times in one paragraph (Matthew 5:6-7). Jesus did not say, "*If* you pray," but "*When* you pray." Jesus' followers are to be people of prayer. Prayer is not an optional aspect of Christian living. However, in seasons of depression, our normal mode of prayer may not seem to help.[50] Consider changing your approach.

### Prayers for When You Cannot Pray

At times, depression has left me with no words for God. I did not know what to say. Nor, did I have the will-power or energy to dig

---

[50] Keen, P. 101.

out the elusive words. But, prayer is an aspect of Christian life that must happen even when the Christian has no words.

My best solution, one now shared with thousands, is using the Psalms as a prayer book. Instead of silently reading the words of the Psalms, I read those same words aloud.

Author Eugene Peterson said silent reading was never the intent of the psalms. He argues that the psalms were written to be spoken aloud. While reading silently, particularly material with which we are already familiar, our eyes tend to flow over the words without mental engagement.

Something different happens when the same sentences are read aloud. Slowly reading the words aloud engages the mind. In this context, the mouth cannot speak unless the brain is fully engaged. When I read the Psalms in this manner, it is only a short time before I encounter a Psalm that expresses my current experience. At that moment, the ancient psalm becomes my present prayer. It has spoken my situation to my Lord. My feelings have been expressed to Him.

**Step by Step Directions on Praying the Psalms**

Here is how this works for me.

1. Open the Bible to Psalm 1.
2. Slowly read Psalm 1 aloud.
3. If something in Psalm 1 connects to my life situation, I claim it as my prayer. I will likely read the Psalm again. Perhaps reading it several times.
4. If Psalm 1 does not speak to my life situation, I'll read Psalm 2 in the same way. If it connects, that Psalm is claimed as my prayer. It is my practice to do as was portrayed in #3 above.
5. If Psalm 2 does not connect, move on to Psalm 3.
6. I'll continue to read Psalms aloud slowly until something connects. I've not yet read ten psalms without coming to that sense of connection.

At that moment, when I could not pray because I had no words, God's psalmist had already written the needed words.

At times, praying the Psalms aloud has brought me to strong emotion. It is the realization, "Somebody has been in this state of mind before me. I'm not the first person to be here."

In your relationship with Jesus, don't search for words that won't come. Instead, read the inspired words of the psalmist. When you follow this approach, you won't feel as though your prayer is an ineffective waste.[51]

## Prayer Journaling

In one of my absolute darkest seasons of depression, I gained a valued practice. I was reading through the book *Too Busy Not To Pray*. The author described a particular approach to prayer journaling. It was simple, yet effective.

There are five portions:

1. *Remembrance* – A paragraph devoted to thinking about and writing about the events of yesterday. The goal of remembrance is to get you to slow down and become introspective. I write my "remembrance" paragraph in the back of my journal. So this simple diary travels from the back of the book toward the front.
2. *Adoration* – A paragraph focused on exalting a single attribute of the Lord Jesus Christ.
3. *Confession* – A paragraph that confesses sins, needs and dependence on Him.
4. *Thanksgiving* – A paragraph expressing appreciation for things Jesus has done in my life and family.
5. *Supplication* – This paragraph is for my intercession and requests about specific things.

The prayer part of the daily journaling starts at the front of the journal.

Let me flesh this out. If you choose to try this, you will adopt the prayer journal approach by taking the following steps.

---

[51] A companion book *Songs for the Dark Place* by Norma and I is a compilation of Psalms that seem to most often speak to the dark moments of life. Information about it can be found at CarltonCoonSr.com

1. Get a journal. My first journals were simple spiral bound notebooks. My current journals are a bit more elegant. The spiral bound notebook worked just as well.
2. Each day, go to the back of the journal. Write down the date. Now draft a bit of a diary of yesterday's events. Your remembrance is to be no more than a single paragraph. Six sentences are enough. The goal is to slow down and engage your mind. You can't rush proper prayer.
3. Now go to the front of your journal. Again, put the date at the top of the page.
4. Now you are ready for "A" for *Adoration*. This paragraph, likely a bit longer than your paragraph of remembrance, will express adoration and appreciation for a single aspect of the nature of the Lord Jesus Christ.

   1. The idea of what to "*adore*" him for each day does not naturally flow to me.
   2. I use devotional books or books I adapt to use as devotional material. Some of the books I've used include the five books by Charles Rolls that describe God in short snippets. Rolls often offers profound revelation.
   3. F.B. Meyer and G. Campbell Morgan both wrote books which include a few paragraphs about a single verse in each chapter of the Bible. These books have been helpful resources for this part of my prayer.
   4. As I read, the first topic written by Rolls, Meyer, Morgan, etc. may not resonate as a topic I'd like to celebrate.
   5. When this is the case, I read another; if necessary, I continue reading until a concept about the nature of God that deserves my adoration gains my attention.
   6. I then write my expression of adoration of Jesus. My focus is on one attribute. Praying like this has brought me to a place of knowing Jesus better.

5. C is for Confession. This half-page makes me look at myself. I often engage the Lord Jesus as my advocate. The appeal for His advocacy happens here.

    1. There are sins to confess.
    2. There are also times when I confess to being over my head and in need God's wisdom and direction.

6. T is for Thanksgiving. Depression focuses on the bad. Nothing is good. The depressed person feels they have never accomplished anything worthwhile. No good thing has come their way. Life stinks. In reality, this is all untrue. Life does not stink. There is much for which to be thankful. Writing a half-page of thanksgiving to the Lord helps.
7. S is for Supplication. The final half-page is where appeals are made to God. Occasionally, I'll look back at journals from fifteen years ago and realize how often Jesus has answered prayer.

What does this model of prayer have to do with depression? This model, and others like it, force me toward thoughtful prayer. Jesus opposed praying with "vain repetition." (Matthew 6:7) Praying with vain repetition is a wandering mind connected to a moving mouth.

Depressed people need tools to cause them to "think about what they are thinking about." Prayer journaling accomplishes this.

Having a good prayer meeting, or even "praying through" seldom ends the depression." How I wish it did. However, the practice of prayer is not feeling-based. Nor is prayer an optional exercise. As Christians we are to pray when we feel like it and we are to pray when we don't feel like it. Depressed people are to pray, even if prayer does not provide immediate deliverance from the pain.

# Chapter 24
# Seek Counsel

Counseling can help overcome depression. Wise counsel benefits on many fronts. Through the years, our family has repeatedly benefitted from family counsel. Professional counselors who are not preachers have also helped.

Some years back, I completed a yearlong course on pastoral counseling. My reading and the bit of education taught me two things:

- How little I knew about addressing complex issues like sexual abuse and ongoing marital discord. Spiritual or Biblical decisions are in my comfort zone. Beyond, responding to issues by saying, "The Bible Says . . . !" the word *Band-aid* describes my counsel. A *Band-aid* can help many situations, but it won't heal major trauma.
- That some in the field of mental health, including some Christian counselors, do not understand the wisdom of the Bible. This is unfortunate. The Bible contains wisdom from God. Such wisdom is to be applied.

My response to this new information about counseling was to seek help. Several Christian counselors were recommended to me for their use of Biblical wisdom. When my counseling *Band-Aid* will not do, I refer people to one of these counselors.

## The Biblical View of Counsel

The idea of seeking counsel is not new. The Bible is emphatic regarding the value of counsel. A few texts, with commentary will suffice.

*Where no counsel is, the people fall:*
*but in the multitude of counsellors there is safety.*
**Proverbs 11:14**

The Hebrew word translated *counsel* was a nautical term. The word referred to ropes tied to a ship to safely guide it the last few yards into a port. Getting a ship safely into port is meticulous work not left to chance. A paraphrase might read: *Where no steerage is, no ropes tied to guide their ship, the people will fall.*

In the verse, a different Hebrew word is then translated *counselors,* "**. . . in the multitude of counselors there is wisdom.**" This word means to deliberate. Deliberation indicates thoughtfulness. A good counselor does not "shoot from the lip." The counselors makes an intentional effort to "form a design."[52] The counselor listens then *forms a design* to help get a person safely "into port."

Solomon said there is safety in such counsel. The word "safety" also gives insight. Strong's Concordance's second English definition of the Hebrew word indicates this "safety" means *to be rescued.* A good counselor can rescue and keep people from crashing as a result of depression.

Other passages affirm the value of counsel.

> *Without counsel purposes are disappointed:*
> *but in the multitude of counsellors they are established.*
> **Proverbs 15:22**

### Why Counsel Matters

Only a fool sees themselves as beyond needing wise advice. The need for counsel is more acute for those who for the first time deal with Major Depressive Disorder.

Depression causes us to look inward. Those looking inward are not looking around for someone who might be able to help.[53] This is unfortunate, because a depressed person could well need a trained counselor to help him heal.

Why is there benefit from a professional counselor?

1.  They don't know you. It is hard to be transparent with someone who leads in worship or preaches to you. None of us want our pastor to know everything about us!

---

[52] Wilson, William; *Wilson's Old Testament Word Studies.* (Peabody, MA, Hendrickson Publishers), P.98.

[53] Meir, Paul M.D., Arterburn, Stephen M. Ed., Minirth, Frank M.D., *Mastering Your Moods* (Nashville, Tennessee, Thomas Nelson, 1999) P. 143.

2. A qualified counselor uses techniques to help you recognize when you are not being truthful with yourself.
3. A counselor is there to help. A counselor never ridicules, judges, or condemns.
4. The counselor is unbiased in their ability to appraise your behavior. A counselor can ask questions that make you think about your behavior and life in a different light.[54]
5. Professional counselors cost money. The counselor may have a sliding scale based on income, but there is a cost. When we spend our money, we tend to value what is being done. Every professional counselor I've worked with has given homework. Not completing this work would have caused the entire thing to be a waste of time and money. Having a bill to pay makes the process more important.

As is true with other solutions, counseling is not an immediate fix. Minirth and Meier say the typical patient will need about fifty hours of counseling to dissolve a Major Depressive Disorder.[55] This is a major commitment, but necessary and beneficial.

**Finding a Counselor**

There has to be a relatively comfortable relationship between the people in any counseling relationship. Two times, I did not continue sessions because the counselor and I didn't connect.

Being comfortable does not mean you will like what the counselor says or what you are directed to do. Being in counsel is hard work. Often, you will leave the counselor's office feeling worse than when you entered. It is similar to having a minor out-patient surgery. When you leave the surgeon's office, there is discomfort, but the surgery has provided a necessary remedy. Counseling can be painful.

If your pastor is amenable and knowledgeable about this sort of counsel, ask him for a recommendation. Otherwise, several websites

---

[54] Sutton and Hennigan P. 144
[55] Meir, Arterburn, Minirth P 150.

list Christian counselors and their area of expertise. There are often online reviews of what it is like to work with a particular counselor.

Technology now allows counseling via Skype, FaceTime or other video links. Your counselor need not be in your city or country. For some people, a counselor being at a distance increases the level of comfort.

## What to Expect in Counseling Sessions

Every counselor approaches their work in a different way. To give a specific outline of what will happen in your counseling sessions will likely disappoint you and cause you to question my credibility. There are some general things to expect.

Counselors' offices are arranged to maintain privacy. On arrival, you will likely enter a small waiting room. When you leave the counselor's office, you may exit by a different door. The second exit reduces the likelihood of you encountering an acquaintance.

Your counselor will request the same information as any doctor. In many instances, the counselor's practice comes under the Health Insurance Portability and Accountability **Act**. (HIPPA). You will sign the same sort of forms as when you visit any doctor.

An information sheet will almost certainly ask for information about your health – physically, mentally, and emotionally.

You will provide information about your insurance and may be required to make a payment.

The ethical codes of the counselor's profession, requires that any information you share be kept confidential. If the counselor divulges information you share during counsel, they put themselves at risk of losing their professional credentials, as well as facing litigation.

There are generally three exceptions to the last paragraph. These exceptions may vary by state, province and country.

1. If a person is suicidal, the counselor must contact the proper authorities.
2. If you indicate a high likelihood of harming someone else, the counselor is to notify the authorities about this concern.
3. If anyone speaks of having sexually abused a minor, or a minor speaks of having been abused, the counselor (or a

pastor) is required to report this information to the authorities. To protect that child and other children, this information must be given to the state or provinces equal to the Division of Family Services.

Beyond these exceptions, what you say in the counselor's office stays in the counselor's office.

## Inside the Counselor's Office

A counselor's office is usually either sound-proofed or has sound blocking machines. People in another room will not hear what is said.

Your counselor wants to help you. Their first goal will be to make you comfortable. Coffee, tea or water may be offered. There is not likely to be a great deal of small talk, but time will be taken to get acquainted.

Eventually, the counselor will ask questions in an attempt to learn more about your issues. The counselor will likely make notes. The notes will be used to develop follow-up questions and later remind the counselor of what has been discussed.

In time, more questions or an assessment will be used to quantify your depression. The counselor will want to learn the severity of your condition.

A common counseling approach is *cognitive therapy*. The word "cognitive" relates to the mental processes of perception, memory, judgment, and the choices we make. Cognitive therapy hopes to deal with negative emotions by consciously changing the way we think.[56]

Synonyms for *cognitive* include the words: reasoning, mental, intellectual, cerebral, perceptive, rational, etc. These words all refer to the mental processes of daily life. This comes into play with Major Depressive Disorder, because in some instances, depression is a result of improper thought processes. MDD also negatively affects a person's ability to think clearly. The late motivational author Zig Ziglar referred to such thought processes as, "stinking thinking."

---

[56] Sutton and Hennigan, P. 143 – 144.

Cognitive therapy aims to help you *re-think* life. The counselor is unlikely to immediately address your emotional condition and reactions. "Thinking better" helps dampen our emotional reactions to life and leads to making better decisions.

Where there is "stinking thinking," life will be handled in the wrong way. By contrast, healthy thinking gives emotional balance and helps us make better choices. Don't be impatient with the process; a counselor follows a course of action that will lead to long term results.

**More than "Just a Talk"**

Using the tools he is equipped to use, the counselor will guide the conversation. Probing questions will be asked. These can be uncomfortable. From long experience, counselors know that most of us do not initially tell the whole story.

*Counseling that brings healthy inner healing is both painful and exhausting.* A counselor scrapes away mental and emotional scabs that have kept a person from being healthy. This happens as the counselor asks difficult questions and gives you work to do. Often, you will leave the office feeling worse than when you entered.

This work addresses distorted thoughts that may contribute to your depression. The Bible talks about the *renewing of our mind* (Romans 12:2) and having *the mind of Christ* (1 Corinthians 2:16). Does an honest assessment of our thoughts show that our mind is not renewed or like Christ? Our thought processes can change for either good or bad.

1. Such counseling helps you understand your thought process in general or how you are thinking about a particular thing.
2. The counselor may help you come up with alternatives to your current way of thinking.

**Beyond the Counseling Session**

If your counselor uses cognitive therapy, he may encourage you to, "think about what you are thinking about." You could be asked to keep a simple diary to track what you are thinking about.

The homework could be, "I want you to think about . . . And write down the reason you respond in the way you have described to me today." To a point, your commitment to overcoming depression will show in your having done such exercises. The practice of, "thinking about what you are thinking about," should become a habit for any person battling depression.

As we deal with life's decisions, do we step back and ask, "Jesus, what would You have me do?" When a person asks that question, a Bible principle will often come to mind. Those who are thoughtful enough to make choices by Biblical principles will make right decisions regardless of the state of their emotions.

Appointments with a counselor tend to happen one time every 2 or 3 weeks. At times a counselor may feel a weekly appointment is best.

## Learn to H.A.L.T.

Your counselor may teach you to use of the acronym H.A.L.T. as a self-assessment tool. If you are battling depression and it suddenly seems to worsen, do a quick H.A.L.T. self-evaluation. Think about your condition just now. Are you:

- Hungry
- Angry
- Lonely
- Tired

The presence of any one of the H.A.L.T. conditions tends to increase the symptoms of depression. If more than one of the four is present, the likelihood that depression will worsen increases dramatically.

When you notice an increase in the symptoms of depression, ask yourself, "When was the last time I ate?" If it has been longer than a couple of hours, eat something. Get some calories in your body and then reassess your feelings. It is amazing how often these four things: hunger, anger, loneliness, and being tired increase the level of depression.

## Get Help!

If you are depressed, find help. Jesus has made available the gift of counsel. It is foolish to reject a gift God has made available to you.

# Chapter 25
# The Sound of Music

King Saul exhibited classic signs of depression. His depression was, in part, due to his poor decisions. When David played music on the harp, Saul felt better. (1 Samuel 16:23) The "evil spirit" departed.

It seems Saul was onto something. It was a common practice for ancient Greek philosophers to use hymns played on a stringed instrument known as a dulcimer as therapy for people dealing with depression.

After World War II, thousands of soldiers suffering from post-traumatic stress disorder were institutionalized due to being unable to function in society. In those times the unfortunate phrase used for the worst cases of the condition was, "shell shock." In the same era that these soldiers were being institutionalized, theories had been developed showing that music could help with both physical and emotional trauma.

Community musicians decided to test some of these new theories. They started visiting the "shell shocked" soldiers in the institutions. The musicians came and played hymns and soothing melodies for the patients. Soon, nurses and doctors began to notice improved physical and emotional responses in their patients. Traditional therapies had not achieved the same sort of results. This new insight resulted in hospitals actually hiring musicians to improve the recovery rates of patients suffering from extreme trauma.[57]

The American Music Therapy Association is the world's largest music therapy association. Their website describes more than a dozen studies showing the benefits of music for people suffering from depression and anxiety. Some of the documented results include:

- Reduced muscle tension
- Increased self-esteem
- Decreased anxiety and agitation

---

[57] www.everydayhealth.com; "*How Music Therapy Can Relieve Depression;*" By Therese Borchard. May 4, 2017. (Read February 16, 2019)

- Increased verbalization
- Enhanced interpersonal relationships
- Increased motivation
- Successful and safe emotional release.[58]

Tim LaHaye's book on overcoming depression suggests music as a significant help in the battle. My musical ability is limited. I cannot go to a keyboard and play music to express my feelings. Of course, there are times when ferociously playing a set of drums is helpful.

As a norm, music is not playing in my car or office. My day does not usually start with music. I have no "playlist." Perhaps, I should. When I've taken advantage of it, music has been a help to me.

My music for seasons of depression won't have lyrics. Lyrics require more mental focus than I have to give. Instead, Gospel Smooth Jazz, Dinner Jazz or Piano Classics work well for me. At times, some quartet music or gospel tunes from the 1970s and 80s is included. My wife's lone album recorded in the early 80s has also helped.

The genre of music that benefits you will likely differ. The "blues," harsh sounds, or country music portraying the singer crying in his beer is not likely to be a help.

Music won't remedy depression, but it can be an aid. Tomorrow, try turning off the television or talk radio as background noise. Instead, put a background of pleasant music into your mind.

## Oh . . . and Sing

Not being able to hold a key or read a note does not mean you cannot sing. An old question asks, "Do you sing because you are happy, or are you happy because you sing?" I have no answer for the question. My experience is that depression is momentarily put on hold when I sing.

Our home has a bit of land. Enough that a tractor or large mower is needed. This noisy equipment and the shower have been the

---

[58] www.musictherapy.org; "Music Therapy and Mental Health; 2006. (Read February 16, 2019).

setting for me singing at the top of my lungs. Sing – whether you sing well or not.

Music and singing can help in your battle against depression.

# Chapter 26
## Someone Else's Problems

Depression causes an *Elijah Syndrome*. We isolate and turn inward. Elijah had accomplished significant things, but he became convinced no other prophet existed.

People in pain, including the pain of depression, feel their pain to be uniquely different. Author John Powell asked a psychiatrist, "How can you teach people to love?" The psychiatrist answered the question with a question, "Did you ever have a toothache? Of whom were you thinking during the distress of your toothache?"[59] People in pain focus on themselves. It is hard to show love when you are looking inward.

Those battling depression tend to move inside themselves. The will to do something to benefit others is not there. The *Elijah Syndrome* lives on.

An old folk story illustrates a method to overcome the *Elijah Syndrome*. Seraphim of Russia was an elder in the Eastern Orthodox Church. He lived in the mid-1700s. Seraphim spent years living in a cabin praying. His presence was calming to those in his community. Seraphim usually had healing words for those who visited him.

In a village near Seraphim's cabin, a woman's only child; a little boy, had died. So devastating was her pain that she shut out her loss. The woman refused to have her son buried. Claiming her son was not dead, she went through the village saying, "Surely there is a medicine that can cure him."

Eventually, her disconnect was such that she carried her son's dead body about with her. She was angry and said to everyone, "You are hiding the healing medicine from me." Finally a shopkeeper told her, "Go see Seraphim, he may have the medicine for you."

It gave the grieving mother hope. Quickly she went to Seraphim asking for medicine for her son. Seraphim said, "Go to the homes in the village; find one house that has not known sorrow, deep tragedy

---

[59] Powell, John, S.J. *Why am I Afraid to Love*, (Allen, Texas; Argus Communication, 1982) P.25

or loss; get a grain of barley from that house, and bring it to me. I will make the medicine of it. That medicine will heal your son."

With anticipation, the grieving mother did as Seraphim instructed. She went from house to house, asking if their home had experienced no sorrow. She found that not a single home had not known sorrow. Instead, the woman heard people's stories of loss and the great grief in their life. Gradually the mother did not feel alone in her pain. She began to feel her neighbor's pain. Her pain seemed less significant to her when seen as part of the pain everyone else felt.

In time, she returned to Seraphim and said, "I have found no one that has not known tragedy." In the meantime, she had permitted her dead son to be buried. She had changed for the better; the woman was no longer isolated by denial.[60]

Knowing the pain of others helps put life in perspective. Take a 360 degree look around you. No one you see will have escaped grief. No person gets out of life unscarred.

Those who repeatedly battle depression may benefit from volunteering at a hospital or nursing home. Spend time with latchkey kids who are scarcely cared for. Join "Big Brothers" of America or a similar effort. Those who get involved beyond themselves will more quickly find light in their darkness.

---

[60] Ensley, Eddie. *Prayer that Heals Our Emotions* (Columbus, Georgia; Contemplative Books, 1986) P. 92

# Chapter 27
# Clean Up, Dress Up

Depression can make a person sloppy. When a friend who dresses with precision begins to be unkempt, the person may be battling depression.

Depressed people ask themselves, "Why shower? Even if I smell, I'm not going to get near enough anyone for them to smell me." Depressed people retreat into a wardrobe of dingy housecoats or ragged jeans. During times of depression, well-worn pajamas may be the most oft-used part of a person's wardrobe.

Someone unkempt, unwashed, and slouchy may be making a statement about their emotional condition. The look is not just "comfortable." It is that person's outward presentation of their inner reality.

Those who have not experienced an extended bout of MDD will not understand. A depressed person, finds it hard to do anything that is not essential. There are times when getting up, bathing, and dressing in the morning takes more faith and determination than a healthy person will require for a month.[61]

Even when you are depressed, if you wear some of your better clothes and your hair is combed, you are more likely to see yourself in a positive light. Clothes do not make you who you are, but they do have a great deal to say about how you feel about yourself.[62]

## Fight Back

Fight back by making yourself do three things.

1. Each morning, get out of bed and into the shower. Brush your teeth. Comb your hair.
2. Get dressed in the most attractive clothes you have for that day's situations. Even if you are staying home, pajamas or a housecoat won't help you overcome depression. What would

---

[61] Maughon p. 78
[62] Thomas, p. 61

you want to be wearing if your pastor came calling? If life takes you to the office or workplace, wear the absolute best you have. People who make an effort to look their best are fighting the darkness.

3. The late J.T. Pugh advised young preachers, "Stand tall." As you fight depression, don't slouch. Get squarely on your feet with your shoulders back. For a time, you may have to actually think about it to get your shoulders back.

## Take Inventory

In the battle with depression, there are times when doing a few simple things begins the path to recovery. Some of these simple things become enjoyable as we realize this is making a difference for both today and the future. You can begin working on these things today.

- Are you still wearing the same clothes you wore five years ago? If so, purge your closet. You will likely get an emotional lift from this.
- Are your shoes polished? Are your clothes clean and well-pressed? If your shoes are scuffed and scarred – shine them! Get out the iron and ironing board. Use the iron on your shirt or blouse.

Don't let this suggestion drive you deeper into depression. You can accomplish looking nice without spending a lot of money. Macy's, Saks Fifth Avenue and designer labels are not necessary.

A friend who has served in major corporate leadership dresses impeccably. The majority of his wardrobe – including Armani suits is bought on eBay. He spends pennies on the dollar to the clothes' original cost.

Some days when there is nothing significant on my schedule, I have worn my best and newest suit. I wasn't wearing it for someone else. It was for me! I needed every possible aid to feel better about myself. I was battling the darkness.

So - in your battle with depression - dress up.

# Chapter 28
# Tom Barnes' Advice - Talk to Yourself

No, I mean it! Talk to yourself. We all *listen* to ourselves. Much of what we hear is negative.

- You are too fat.
- You are losing your hair.
- How could you be so stupid?

Author Joyce Landorf wrote of *basement voices*. These voices from past and present whisper words of discouragement. No person but you can hear your *basement voices*. From the subconscious you hear, "If only you had more faith . . . If you were praying the right prayer . . . If you were more Godly . . . If you hadn't . . . If you were a true saint, you could hold it all together . . . if, if, if..." And in it all, there is guilt, despair, and a sense of tragic loss.

*Basement voices* give no suggestion for improvement. There is no grace or mercy in the words. Such voices prosecute; they never liberate.

Eliminating the basement voices is a challenge. The *basement voices* build a case against our intelligence, wisdom, integrity, and faith. The "self-talk" becomes an unending stream of negativity. Negative self-talk is a consistent characteristic in those who battle depression.

## Add a Second Voice

Decades ago, Norma and I were itinerant evangelists. During summer, revival opportunities were slim. I'd often work at a youth camp in Louisiana. Those camps allowed me to become acquainted with the late T.W. Barnes. Tom Barnes was a man uniquely used of God. He served as the camp principal for many years.

T. W. Barnes was accessible to young preachers. One day we were alone in a meeting room. It was a God-moment. I shared with him my pre-disposition toward melancholy. At the time, *depression* was not a word in my vocabulary.

Pastor Barnes, whose faith was legendary, surprised me. He told me he dealt with the same challenge. Tom Barnes said, "On the days when I'm not in the right frame of mind, I give myself a good talking to. As I look in the mirror while shaving, I tell myself, 'Tom, you are not going to think that way. That is wrong thinking. You are going to get dressed and get the things done you need to do.'"

T.W. Barnes had dry humor and a wry grin. With that grin he said, "You'll think it is funny, but I stand there and give myself a good talking to." As was the case in praying the psalms, the talk he described was spoken aloud.

The basement voices are silent voices. Even in their silence, they are powerful. But, those silent voices speaking into your mind are not as powerful as the words you speak aloud. The tongue, your tongue has the power of life and death (Proverbs 18:21). I'm not suggesting a "blab it and grab it" sort of talk. Instead, speak aloud:

- Of your plans and intentions for the day.
- Of God's Word your pastor preached the past week.
- A memory of victory in a similar time.
- Faith in God's divine providence and process.

For decades, I have followed Tom Barnes' advice. Those fighting depression would do well to also follow his advice.

Whether you know it or not, the basement voices are constantly whispering. Another voice must be heard. The second voice has words of faith and determination.

To overcome depression, a person must decide to like themselves. We only listen to someone we like. Those are the opinions and perspectives we trust. Lloyd Rosen, who battled depression, wrote, "I never felt like I was worth anything . . . Now I can spend time with myself alone."[63]

You won't win over depression every day, but each day should involve a battle. Using all resources available, including talking to yourself, improves the chances of progress.

---

[63] Rosen, Lloyd S., *Resurrection from Depression*; (CreateSpace; January 2016) p.74

Thinking that reinforces depression is one-sided. The description of our failure, lacking, and inability is a monologue. When we talk back to those basement voices, it at least becomes an argument.

# Chapter 29
# Medicine for the Mind

No information in this chapter is intended to be a substitute for professional medical advice, diagnosis or treatment. It is for information only. No specific medication is recommended. Various medication affects different people in different ways. Always seek the advice of your physician or another qualified health provider with any questions about your medical condition and/or current medication. Do not disregard professional medical advice or delay seeking advice or treatment because of anything you read here.

Depression can be survived! No person's solution will be the same. Survival may well require different approaches for each person.

Let's consider medicine for depression. Based on my experience with anti-depressants, we need a rational, reasoned and logical perspective on their use.

## Anti-depressant Medicine is Seldom the First Option

Some time back, a co-worker was diagnosed with diabetes. With that diagnoses came warnings and options for treatment. The diabetes was at a stage where the doctor hoped to address it without insulin. Doctors take a similar approach in dealing with:

- High blood pressure
- High cholesterol
- Heart disease
- Dozens of other diseases

Medication is not always the first option. A doctor may say, "Let's see if we can address this with a better diet, losing a few pounds, reducing your fat-intake, increasing your exercise, or taking this particular vitamin."

Depression is another condition where a trip to the pharmacy is preferably not the first option.

Let's restate information found earlier in this book.

- Too few neurotransmitters in the brain can cause Major Depressive Disorder.
- Neurotransmitters are biochemicals in the brain.
- These particular chemicals are the result of a natural biological process.
- These neurotransmitters act as bridges facilitating interaction between brain cells.
- When our body is not producing enough of these chemicals, there is an emotional downturn, and physical activity slows. It is as though a bridge normally having two lanes suddenly has only one lane open.

One answer to addressing depression is making sure there are more of these neurotransmitters in the brain.

Several strategies to survive and overcome depression have been mentioned. What if none of these work? Is a depressed person to accept being an emotional vegetable? Are that person's children to endure life with a mentally and emotionally absent parent?

What if medicine could help? High cholesterol, low blood pressure, diabetes, and countless other conditions have been treated by medication. In all of the mentioned diseases, one individual may benefit from a particular medicine while another person is not helped by that same medication. No particular medicine is a guarantee for correcting a heart condition. Neither is any specific medicine guaranteed to help with depression.

Though a particular treatment holds no guarantee, would we expect a diabetic to receive no care until lapsing into a coma? Would we say to a man with high cholesterol, "Sir, a medicine could help, but don't take medicine. Instead, hang on for a miracle. If healing does not come, die with clogged arteries." Such reasoning has been part of earlier Christian history. At one time, some religious leaders warned against even the use of eyeglasses. Their thinking, "If God wanted you to have better vision, He would give it to you." A few cult groups continue such reasoning.

## Could We Treat Depression as an Illness?

Depression is real. Depression is dangerous. Depression can be deadly. Ignoring depression has resulted in substance abuse, domestic violence, rage, long-term hospitalization, and homes tainted with unspeakable misery.

The suicide rate continues to increase. Depression is the underlying reason for suicide.

As someone who has benefited from both professional counseling and quality medical care, I see it all as a gift from God. I'd hate to imagine that any such good gift would be withheld from a person who could benefit.

When depression is a result of chemical imbalance; when "the bridges are down to one lane;" help may come from taking an anti-depressant. The medical field has numerous options. As is the case with heart disease or lupus, a treatment that works for one person won't work for someone else. Thus, the many possible options.

Taking anti-depressants is seldom a permanent thing. The use of medicine may last only a few months. Eventually, depression begins to lift, and the mental "bridges are all open."

## An Approach to Consider

If you have symptoms of depression, you might think of taking the following approach:

1. Consider how long you have been experiencing the symptoms.
2. Educate yourself by reading all you can about depression.
3. Pray. Do ask Jesus to give you complete and instant healing.
4. If healing does not come and the depression does not lift, visit a doctor. Your normal family doctor is a good place to start. Primary care physicians are trained to recognize and treat depression.
5. Visiting a medical doctor is important. Illnesses other than depression can have similar symptoms. A friend had the

symptoms of depression. In reality, the problem was a thyroid condition having nothing to do with his mind.

6. Your doctor will likely have you complete a questionnaire to determine the level of your emotional and mental duress.

7. After reviewing your assessment and asking further questions, the doctor may wish to immediately prescribe medicine. If depression is so intense as to have you on the verge of being suicidal, take the prescription and use it.

8. If the depression is less severe, ask him to suggest other possibilities that have helped lift people out of depression. He may suggest exercise and some of the other options mentioned in this book.

My experience with the "dark place" of depression has taken me to:

- Several primary care physicians
- Three counselors
- Two short-term experiences with psychiatrists. One was a terrible experience, the second was better.

## A Cautionary Note

Modern medical care has often become a bit like a trip through a drive-through window at a fast-food restaurant.

A recent visit to a physician was disappointing. The experience was hurried. He had no time to listen to my story. The doctor did not invite me to ask questions about the proposed treatment. Nor did he explain the objective of the medicine or any potential side-effects. Unfortunately, what the doctor prescribed, at no fault of his own, had intolerable side-effects. It is simply the way this sort of medication works. A medicine that helps one person does not work for another person with the same symptoms.

On my second (and last) visit, I told the doctor my concern over the lack or interaction. The doctor told me his employer required him to see 3-4 patients per hour. His solution to my bad experience with the previous medicine was to quickly write another prescription. I never filled the second prescription. My experience with that one doctor rushing me to the pharmacy may be the 1 in 10,000 such experiences. In our era of managed health care this is likely not the case.

## Other Options First

We are in a "prescription culture." Medicine is big business. Pharmaceutical companies need doctors to prescribe their products. It is how they make money and provide a return to investors.

Pharmaceutical companies constantly promote, market, and pander their product to physicians. In some instances, generally illegally, doctors have received kickbacks for prescribing a particular company's products.

As a patient, you, not your doctor and certainly not a pharmaceutical company, are the decision maker. A product developed by a pharmaceutical company need not be seen as the first step in recovery.

Taking an anti-depressant without having tried some other remedy may not be your best solution. An anti-depressant prescribed by a doctor fulfilling his scheduling requirements is almost certainly never the best approach.

## Is an Anti-Depressant Right for You?

I cannot answer that. Only you, your family, and physician can answer the question. Some people battling depression are pressured or shamed for even considering medical help. Someone says, "You are tougher than that. Don't be such a wimp. Just go pray through."

If you are depressed and this is the sort of "advice" you receive, find other, "wise counsel." What you have heard is not wise counsel. Find a wise friend, family member, or religious leader who will listen. Hopefully that person will have enough life experience to know the realities of depression. If they do, they will likely emphasize the importance of the sound advice of a professional.[64]

---

[64] Keen p. 84

## Questions to Ask the Doctor

Visiting a doctor is stressful. In stressful situations, we may forget important information. Prepare yourself. Since it is easy to forget important information, have the following items with you:

1. A list of medicine you currently take, including over-the-counter or homeopathic remedies.
2. A list of current symptoms and maladies.
3. Your list of potential questions.

As you address depression with your doctor, you may want to take a semblance of this list of questions:

- Other than prescribing medicine, what can you suggest that may help me?
- Do you see my situation as needing medical treatment, counseling, or both?
- How safe is the medication you plan to prescribe?
- What are the side-effects of this medicine? If the side effects bother me, is there another medicine available?
- How long will it take for me to see improvement?
- What are the options if this does not work?
- Will this medicine interact with other medicine I already take?
- How will the medicine affect other medical conditions with which I deal?[65]

## What Anti-depressants Will and Won't Do

Antidepressants do not generate a buzz or "high." Not even close! There is no rush. No thrilling vibes. No living in la-la land. An antidepressant is not LSD. An anti-depressant is not "speed."

Working properly, antidepressants will help your body create those neurotransmitter bridges that allow effective communication between brain cells. The medication allows a person to make focused decisions, and to be a wife, mom, husband, father, and friend as

---

[65] Sutton and Hennigan p. 54

much as possible. They make sleep possible, though for someone dealing with acute depression, sleep may still be difficult.[66]

Anti-depressants are not known to be addictive. While this is true, any medicine, even an over-the-counter treatment can be psychologically addicting. This occurs when we feel stressed if a particular medicine is not at hand. A person taking the natural remedy melatonin as a sleep aid can become psychologically dependent on being able to take melatonin each night. There is nothing physically addictive about melatonin. Instead, what is being experienced is a sense of mental dependence.

Anti-depressants are merely corrective. Think of the medicine as a diabetic might think of insulin. Insulin is needed to function, and it carries no long-term effects. It is not addictive. Neither are antidepressants.

Such medicine can be a crutch, until a measure of healing has begun. If depression is deep enough, it is almost impossible for a counselor to communicate with a person until the symptoms of depression are brought under some control. Anti-depressant medication can help with this.

## Life While Taking an Anti-Depressant

When you begin taking an antidepressant, in the best case you won't *feel* anything. Anti-depressants are not "speed." If your doctor prescribes an antidepressant, don't mix in your own concoction of homeopathic remedies.

If you do feel anything as a result of taking medicine, what you feel may be unpleasant. Antidepressants are powerful medicine. Most, if not all of them, have side effects. My first experience with taking an antidepressant left me with nausea so severe that I rarely kept the medicine down. If a side effect is significant, contact your doctor.

If you have a bad experience such as over-whelming nausea, don't stop trying to get help. Your doctor has other options. Ask the doctor to try another medicine. You may go through several antidepressants

---

[66] Keen. p. 93

before things begin to work. In some cases, a medicine will have no side-effects. Instead, that particular medicine simply does not work.

Like dealing with many things in the medical field, dealing with depression is an imperfect science.

## It Takes Time

Antidepressants are not a quick fix. An antidepressant is not for your brain like Nyquil is for a cold. Nyquil begins to affect cold symptoms almost immediately. By contrast, in most instances it takes 4-6 weeks for results to come from an anti-depressant.

Taking medicine for a week and deciding it is not working is not the right approach. Be patient. Don't over-medicate. Taking twice the prescribed dosage won't speed your recovery.

Because antidepressants are such a powerful medicine, don't stop taking them suddenly. Your doctor may taper the medicine down when you no longer need the treatment.

# A Final Note

Andrew Solomon's book on depression is well-titled. He called it, *The Noonday Demon*. He wrote:

Depression is a flaw in love. To be creatures who love, we must be creatures who can despair at what we lose. Depression is the mechanism of that despair. When it comes, it degrades one's self and ultimately eclipses the capacity to give or receive affection.

It is the aloneness within us made manifest, and it destroys not only connection to others, but also the ability to be peacefully alone with oneself. Love, though it is no prophylactic against depression, is what cushions the mind and protects it from itself. Medication and psychotherapy can renew that protection, making it easier to love and be loved, and that is why they work.

Do what you must to survive depression! Do what you must without shame! Do what you must without guilt! Find a way to love and be loved.

To learn more about the online training courses, teaching, writing and pastoral ministry of Carlton L. and Norma J. Coon visit Carltoncoonsr.com.

# Bibliography

Biebel, David B. and Koenig Harold G. *New Light on Depression: Help, Hope, and Answers for the Depressed and Those Who Love Them.* (Grand Rapids, Michigan; Zondervan Publishing House, 2003)

Bloomfield, Harold H. M.D., McWilliams Peter. *How to Heal Depression.* (Los Angeles, California; Prelude Press, p. 1996)

DeMeyer, Marian M.D. *The Chemistry of Depression and Suicide* (New York City, New York; The Saturday Evening Post Society, 1982)

Dobbins, Richard D. *Your Spiritual and Emotional Power.* (Ada, Michigan; F.H. Revell Co. 1984)

Ensley, Eddie. *Prayer that Heals Our Emotions.* (Columbus, Georgia; Contemplative Books, 1986)

George, Bob. *Victory Over Depression.* (Eugene, Oregon; Harvest House Publishers, 2001)

Hart, Archibald, *Counseling the Depressed*, Volume 5 from *Resources for Christian Counseling* (Waco, Texas; Word Books, 1987) Gary Collins, General Editor.

Hawkins, David B. *When You're Down With the Blues* (Colorado Springs, Colorado; Cook Communication Ministries, 2001)

Hazard, David. *Breaking Free from Depression (Healthy Body, Healthy Soul).* (Eugene, Oregon; Harvest House Publishers, 2002)

Keen, Bonnie. *A Ladder Out of Depression: God's Healing Grace for the Emotionally Overwhelmed.* (Eugene, Oregon; Harvest House Publishers, 2005)

Kramlinger, Keith. *Mayo Clinic on Depression: Answers to Help You Understand, Recognize and Manage Depression.* (Rochester, Minnesota; Mayo Clinic, 2001)

LaHaye, Tim. *Ten Steps to Victory Over Depression.* (Grand Rapids, Michigan; Zondervan Publishing House, 1980)

Lasagna, Louis. *Learning to Live With Depression.* (New York City, New York; Medicine in the Public Interest, 1994)

Littauer, Florence. *Blow Away the Black Clouds.* (Scottsdale, Arizona; Good Life Productions, 1979)

Mallory, James D. and Hefley, James C. *Untwisted Living.* (Wheaton, Illinois; Victor Books, 1982)

Maughon, Martha. *Why am I Crying? A Personal Look at Depression- One of the Most Serious Problems Facing Women Today.* (Grand Rapids, Michigan; Zondervan Publishing House, 1983)

Meir, Paul M.D., Arterburn, Stephen M. Ed., Minirth, Frank M.D. *Mastering Your Moods.* (Nashville, Tennessee; Thomas Nelson, 1999)

Minirth, Frank, Meier Paul, Meier Richard, Hawkins Don. *Happy Holidays - How to Beat the Holiday Blues.* (Grand Rapids, Michigan; Baker Book House, 1990)

Minirth, Frank, Meier Paul, Meier Richard, Hawkins Don. *The Healthy Christian Life.* (Grand Rapids, Michigan; Baker Book House, 1988)

Mohline, Dick and Jane; *Emotional Wholeness – Connecting with the Emotions of Jesus.* (Shippensburg, Pennsylvania; Treasure House, 1997)

Powell, John, S.J. *Why am I Afraid to Love*. (Allen, Texas; Argus Communication, 1982)

Rosen, Lloyd S. *Resurrection from Depression*. (Scotts Valley, California; Createspace Independent Publishing Platform, 2016)

Sanders, J. Oswald. *Facing Loneliness*. (Crowborough, East Sussex, England; Highland Books, 1988)

Solomon, Andrew. "Anatomy of Melancholy." *The New Yorker* Jan. 1998: 54. Print

Storr, Anthony. *Churchill's Black Dog, Kafka's Mice and Other Phenomena of the Human Mind*. (New York City, New York; Ballantine Books, 1990)

Styron, William. *Darkness Visible: A Memoir of Madness*. (New York City, New York; Vintage Press, 1992)

Sutton, Mark and Henningan, Bruce. *Conquering Depression (A 30 Day Plan to Finding Happiness)*. (Nashville, Tennessee; Broadman & Holman Publishers, 2001)

Thomas, Marian *A New Attitude*. (Shawee, Kansas; National Press Publications, 1991)

Welch, Edward T. *Depression: Looking Up From the Stubborn Darkness*. (Greensboro, North Carolina; New Growth Press, 2011)

White, John. *The Masks of Melancholy*. (Downers Grove, Illinois; Intervarsity Press, 1982)